MEMORY IMPROVEMENT:

Brain Training and Accelerated Learning

Discover Your Unlimited Memory. Potential Declutter Your Mind to Boost Your IQ Through Insane Focus

By Frank Steven

Congratulations on purchasing Memory Improvement:

Remember and Memorize Faster & Better and thank you for doing so!

The following chapters will discuss about how to Remember and Memorize Faster and Better using Cutting-Edge Methods to Improve Your Memory in Just 30 Days.
The information found in this book will best explore topics such as Accelerated Learning, Speed Reading, Photographic Memory, Brain Training and many More. in order for you to understand and improve your memory.

Thanks again for choosing this book! Every effort was made to ensure it is full of as much useful information as possible. Please enjoy!

Table of Contents

Introduction

It is said though that good memory, like a vivid photo that yellows over time, soon fades. How many times have you rushed into a room with purpose and then forget why? How many times have you gone to the grocery store to pick a few items and then realize upon getting home that you forgot to buy the most important item you went to the store for in the first place? Everybody, particularly those hitting late adulthood has these moments.

But young people also fall victim to forgetfulness, missing such important occasions as birthdays and anniversaries or essential information like a telephone number or a street address. We cannot, therefore, swiftly conclude that young and fit people have a monopoly on a good memory. While there are kids that could recite all the non-metal elements in the Periodic Table, or at least parrot the factors of 7 in the multiplication table, there are also individuals in their late adulthood that could easily complete a difficult-level crossword puzzle or utter by heart the Preamble to the Constitution.

It is safe to say that all of us, regardless of age, fall prey to poor memory. The good news is that there are ways we could give our brains the workout it needs to keep our memory as sharp as a surgeon's scalpel.

Chapter 1: Memory And Memory Loss

The brain is truly one of the most amazing organs of the human body. In elementary school, we were taught to think of the brain as the "command center" of the body, as it controls everything from our heart rate, digestive rhythms, to the movement of our fingers and toes. The brain is in charge of intercepting and processing the numerous stimuli that we pick up from our environment, animals, objects, and people. Can you imagine what life would be like if our brains weren't powerful enough to make sense and sort all of the information our body receives in copious amounts? You would be overwhelmed with the minor details of every single object around you if your brain could not sort which details are more important than the rest. However, information processing is only one of the amazing feats that the brain is capable of.

Human memory, as in the ability to create, retain and retrieve memories when they are needed, is a daily miracle. Because we seemingly access memories without exerting extra effort, we underestimate the work of our brain with regards to the memory process. However, for the people who have difficulty remembering important dates, names, and experiences, the memory process can be quite tricky to master. This is true for those who are in the late stages of their lives, and for those who are affected by illnesses or special conditions.

In this chapter, you will learn all about memory- what it is, how it works, and most importantly, what affects or causes memory loss. By the end of this chapter, you should have a deeper understanding of human memory, and be able to apply what you have learned in the following chapters, as well as in your endeavors to avoid memory loss.

What is this thing called memory?

Memory is often referred to as the ability to remember. Whether or not you remember the birthdays of your family members, the emergency phone number of your doctor, the address of your parents, or the time and place of your crucial business meeting all depends on the capacity of your brain to store and access memories. These memories help us learn and adapt to the different situations life presents us with. It is what aids us in learning about the dangers of fire, of over speeding and too much alcohol, or the giddy, happy feeling we associate with the love we receive from relatives and our partners in life. Memories work in that they allow us to remember what we did yesterday, what we need to do today, and what we must do tomorrow. Without memory, our lives would degenerate to a confusing of the loop of frustration and a feeling of incompleteness. Memory is so vital to humans for their survival that science has studied the process of memory-making, as well as advanced techniques individuals can use to boost their mental prowess.

Learning versus memory

It must be made clear that though memory is an important part of learning, the former is not synonymous to the latter. The neurons in our brains behave differently when we learn or experience something for the first time, compared to when we access memories of what we have already learned or previous experience.

For example, a martial artist learns of the different kicks and punches needed in competition through constant practice. The experience of kicking and punching in a certain way triggers a specific group of neurons to fire again and again into the brain, so that the body can make connections with the experience and required movement. Later, once the body has successfully learned or acquired the needed skills for martial arts, it depends on memory to be able to execute the movements once more. Therefore, it can be said that memory is dependent on learning and that learning is the trigger that activates memory. In turn, memory helps our species learn by providing us with a basis of the past on which we can predict the outcome or future path.

How does memory work?

The memory process begins with the encoding phase. This phase relies on all of your five senses to help the brain gather information about a certain object, place, person, or experience. For example, can you still remember what you had for breakfast this morning? Chances are, the first thing that came to your mind when you read the question was the smell or taste of whatever it was that you ate for your first meal today. The smell and taste would have been accompanied by a vivid image of letting us say, a plate of bacon and eggs.

How does memory loss occur?

Two parts of your brain called the hippocampus, and the frontal cortex is responsible for bringing the sensations filtered by your senses to the brain for deciphering and encoding. Neurons constantly fire in your brain and activate the gaps between your nerve cells, called synapses. The repeated activation and electrical impulse activity that occurs in between the synapses are critical to memory making. The more the synapses and other parts of your brain are used constantly, the easier it is for you to remember. This is why repetition often leads to rote memorization of facts. People with intellectual and memory disabilities often have slower synapse responses or no synapse response at all. This means that the information your body is passing along to the brain is hampered, or completely stopped- thus memories fail to form, and memory loss occurs.

What are some of the factors that affect or cause memory loss?

While many factors can cause early or rapid development of

memory loss in certain individuals, scientists and doctors agree that negative stress plays a major role in the destruction or deterioration of neural paths. Other things that affect the creation and the accessing of memories are depression, several medications, a malfunctioning thyroid, menopause or pregnancy, aging, excessive drinking, and mild to severe head traumas.

Chapter 2: Why We Forget Things And Why It Is Important To Have Awesome Memory:

There are all kinds of ways human memory works well or not so well hence Memory is considered to be a very complicated process. Memory is the primary factor behind everything we do like to remember somebody's name or remembering a phone number, from remembering information needed to pass an exam, to remember how to walk or even how to talk.

Memory makes up our continual experience of life and provides us with a sense of self. The hippocampus plays a vital role in memory. We can find the hippocampus in both hemispheres because both sides of the brain are symmetrical. If either side of the hippocampus is destroyed or damaged, as long as the other side is undamaged, memory function will remain nearly normal. Damage to both sides of hippocampus could obstruct the capability to form new memories, called "anterograde amnesia."

Functioning of the hippocampus could also roll down with age. People may have lost as much as 20 percent of the nerve connections in the hippocampus by the time they reach their 80's. However, this neuron loss is not applicable for all the older adults.

Most of the short-term memories are forgotten quickly, and the ability of short-term memory is quite limited. Experts accept as true that you could hold about seven items in short-term memory for approximately 20 to 30 seconds. By using memory approaches like "chunking," this capacity can be stretched somewhat. It involves combination related information into slighter "chunks."

For storing a list of items the capacity of short-term memory was somewhere between five and nine. But today, a lot of memory experts suppose that the actual capacity of short-term memory is most likely nearer to the number four.

By trying out this short-term memory experiment, you can see this in action for yourself. Spend two minutes of time remembering a random list of words, then take a blank piece of a paper and try writing down as many of the words which you can memorize.

Being tested on the information helps you to remember it better. Here is the list of some of the major reasons why we forget the information:

Retrieval Failure: One likely explanation retrieval failure is called "decay theory." As per this theory, every time a new theory is formed a memory trace is created. These memory traces begin to disappear and fade over time. If the information is not rehearsed and retrieved, it will ultimately be lost.

However, one problem with this theory is that if the memories which have not been remembered or rehearsed are amazingly stable in long-term memory.

Interference: This theory suggests that some memories interfere and compete with other memories. Interference is more possible to occur when the information that was previously stored in the memory is very similar to other information

There are two types of interference:

• Retroactive interference occurs when new information gets in the way with your capability to remember previously learned information.

• Proactive interference occurs when an old memory makes it more impossible or difficult to remember a new memory.

Failure to Store: At times, losing information has more to do with the fact that it never made it into long-term memory in the first place and less to do with forgetting. Encoding failures sometimes stop the information from going inside the long-term memory.

Motivated Forgetting: Occasionally, we might vigorously work to forget the memories, particularly those of disturbing events or experiences or traumatic. The two basic types of motivated forgetting are repression, an unconscious form of forgetting and suppression, a conscious form of forgetting.

"How erratic and slow is the growth of a student who cannot even keep in mind what he has learnt."

On the other hand, people with a good working memory are considered to be more self-assured and optimistic, and more likely to direct a successful and happy life. Hence, the use of mnemonic devices could increase memory a lot, especially the recall of long lists of numbers, names, etc.

Benefits and disadvantages of having a good or bad memory:

There is no need to reside on the significance of having a good and sharp memory. A bad remembrance is such a handicap in life that everyone understands the benefits of a good memory. By a good memory, we mean an accurate and retentive memory that would keep hold of the information and retains it appropriately for us.

The chief cause of a bad memory is lack of concentration and inattention. You never really read a book if at once forget all about it. You forget it because your mind was traveling and what the author wrote, you never really took into your mind, your eyes passed over the words on the page.

A good memory is necessary for everyone in every walk of life like the businessman, the student, the statesman, the politician, the employee. For a person who could never remember the faces of those he has met and is not able to recognize his social engagements will not be a social success hence, it is essential in social life too.

Our inability to forget things we do not want to remember is the only disadvantage of a good memory. There are thoughts, events and desires in our life history that we would like to forget. You cannot forget by trying to forget, to fill our mind with good thoughts, is the only way to forget such unpleasant things.

A lot of us believe that if an individual is born with a good memory, he is considered to be lucky. We tend to classify people into two sections:

- Those with a poor memory

- Those with a good memory.

There are two sorts of memory that identify how we remember, and both are essential for learning to occur. These are:

•   Implicit memory: may refer to those things one learns without really thinking about it such as driving a car or breathing.

•   Explicit memory: may refer to the ability of one to deliberately recall particular things like where you last had your car keys or what you had for dinner last night.

We believe that no matter what a person with low memory does, there is no way of improving one's memory capacity and a person having a poor memory is cursed for a lifetime. A very little proportion of world population has a quite good knowledge of how memory works, why most frequently our memory fails us and at times, how we could remember particular things so well.

There are tremendous advantages to having a good memory. To be successful and to be able to learn in life an accurate and retentive memory is essentially needed.

Having a good memory gives one the capability to remember and learn a great range of things fluctuating from such things as life experiences, people, emotions, relationships, skills that he or she has learned, to where that person has parked the car in the parking lot.

Chapter 3: The Ways To Improve Memory

To be able to enhance your memory, you need to utilize it! Actively using your mind is the ideal approach to exercise your brain improve your memory abilities. People with strong memory have some habits which won't miss them daily.

The same thing goes with your memory also. Memory depends on every one of the five senses so that it makes perfect sense to engage every one of them in the brain training approach. Since you may see, gaining a photographic memory is among the things that the majority of us can achieve, and the majority of the methods out there are pretty easy to accomplish from home.

With practice, you are going to be astonished at how much your memory can improve. The mind is a complex function which enables us to recall not only recent events but events from several years past. If you're searching for strategies to increase your memory, odds are you've run into a particular memory improvement technique called repetition, which is intended to assist you in memorizing facts, lists, or numbers. If you would like to increase your memory further, you've got to connect the data that you wish to consider in a manner that is significant to you. If you indeed are sincere in wanting to enhance your memory, you might have to put in the effort and challenging your brain to remember and recall and a high

16

degree of enthusiasm which you can do it. Gaining a photographic memory will offer you an edge in anything you do, and you won't be hindered by any moment of forgetfulness whenever you must recall something crucial at any particular time or situation.

Everybody can enhance their memory. There are two sorts of consciousness. If your memory is exercised, then you might be able to keep in mind the little things you always appear to forget. Possessing an outstanding memory is a gift that you could receive anytime in your life. If you want to have a more powerful mind and be in a position to remember easier there are some memory techniques which you could work on.

Whenever you have enough sleep, your brain is far more alert. Your mind will subsequently make sure it stays in your memory. You would need to tell your brain actively at every given moment that you want to increase your memory abilities.

If you devote quite a bit of time with your pals and socialize with them, you're more likely to come up with a sharp memory. If it comes time to having something to remember you'll be all set for it and you won't have an issue. Among the methods to come up with a sharp memory is to laugh at each opportunity. When you exercise your mind, you're practicing for when you've got to remember. Some excellent strategies for keeping your body together with your account in the absolute best form it can be are to find enough sleep and to exercise on a regular basis. Living a wholesome life also can help you maintain your memory skills longer. It's possible to use real life instead of a picture, for example.

If you'd like to take memory improvement seriously, you may read below for more details. Memory improvement is vital for life instead of to enhance study abilities. To boost memory requires you first to improve concentration and focus.

An important technique to study effectively is to get a guide about what to consider and where to commence. They continue to be a lot of techniques that may help men and women in improving their memory functions. Although association techniques are different and use the exact principals, attempt and make use of what you know works best for you. Thus it is recommended that you implant your associations instead of adopting a foreign system.

Part of obtaining a fantastic diet plan and exercise is to receive a good quantity of sleep. Doing exercise will cause you to slim down and feel more energetic during the day. People need to do regular activities for them to find the most suitable quantity of oxygen which they need. Doing Exercise Doing exercise enables the blood travel to all portions of the body.

If you're not able to handle your stress, you will very soon face memory problems. When you're under pressure for a brief period, you truly improve memory and concentration. Stress can negatively affect brain power.

The above hints will help you remain alert and memorize information once the opportunities require. Unless you concentrate on the news, it won't store. Remembering information can be difficult, in life we are usually just anticipated to remember things, we're never taught anything on how to remember things.

Memory games are an enjoyable way and efficient method to pass the moment. Other folks believe that memory games are just all for improving the memory and others might not feel that it is going to be helpful or beneficial in their day-to-day life. Additionally, there are intellectual games that may boost our knowledge while also, there are memory games that could help our brains become sharper.

HOW TO MAKE YOURSELF PAY ATTENTION

Memory is the ability to retain information. The manhood is useful behind maintaining data from the mind is the mind. The brain has an essential role in memory improvement. Every individual has an account, but you may realize that most individuals do not possess the identical memory quality. Why can it be so? It is a result of the mental aspect which has an integral part in keeping and improving memory. The brain has got great power. An individual must first learn how to use the mind most effectively. For memory improvement, mold your head from the sense; deliver the thought process into command. Meditation aids in soothing the brain, and it also helps in enhancing memory. As soon as you calm down your head, then the mind which has got plenty of capacity may be used for storing information.

Memory Improvement helps improve the future of somebody through livelihood enhancement, thereby the quality of life of an individual also enhances. Enhancing the memory helps you to feel more assured in life. Memory improvement techniques can help one to upgrade the memory.

There are many ways of improving memory. Practice some hints that assist with improving memory. Practice hints like chanting A-U-M (Used in Yoga practice). An exercise of specific yoga's help in memory improvement. This helps in strengthening your mental or memory abilities. The nature of the brain is that the more one uses it, the longer it works. You have to have encounter stage actors who do a lot of memory oriented tasks such as; they function and recall so many things at one time. This is possible by strengthening the memory capacity by immersion technique and by repeated practice. Memory can be increased by using techniques like mind maps, by using model visualizations, meditation, etc..

The basic requirement in memory enhancement techniques is "paying attention" Care can be developed by firm conclusion and reasoning. Paying attention has an essential role in improving memory. Once you generate interest, then you will automatically begin paying attention. To remember something connection that with some events or objects so that you get a succession of events being saved in the memory.

Only if they use, it is going to enhance the memory. First, understand the methods for memory improvement, and then you need to train yourself through continuous practice. Exercise makes you perfect for improving the memory. So practice the technique until it becomes a habit. Gradually you'll undoubtedly find yourself in a better position. Memory works by forming connections from the mind.

FINDING YOUR LEARNING STYLE

Our memory is indeed essential as it helps to maintain those life events in our thoughts for the years to come. Apparently when you remember a memory in 15 years earlier but you forget that the grocery list, it can be so annoying. There are lots of men who want to discover a way that they can improve upon their memory. Well, there are things you can do to help other than merely dealing with frustration more than things you overlook.

It's essential that we have a look at how things are learned earlier we get involved with approaches for memory improvement. When you take part in a brand new experience, or you hear something new, the mind must take that advice and decode it. It requires the data and interprets it in certain ways. Whenever you're focusing on something, and you learn something new, the brain takes the information and documents it.

It's much like putting information into a file cabinet which you open up. As soon as you want to remember that information again, the mind brings it out for you. It's just like walking back to the filing cabinet and regaining the file you put in there before.

Most likely you can remember when your memory was great, and you probably were accustomed to that. When we do not work on keeping our mind in good shape and studying new ways which we can believe our memory ability may begin to slide somewhat. Think about a priest. While she may have spent time training for all her motions, when she stops training, and will not be able to get out there and start performing if she hasn't been practicing for several decades. It is like that with all the memory too.

1 method to improve memory is always to be aware of all that is going on around you. Many individuals only half pay attention when other people talk to them. It's easy to focus on another thing that you need to do instead of what they say. Make sure you begin focusing on what is happening around you so you may keep it and bring it back up later on.

When you receive new information, work to connect it with something that you know to make it much easier to remember. You will find a variety of learning techniques that are different, so see. Others learn from hearing matters.

If you don't know something, find out more about it by studying it all on your own. While it can seem difficult to learn, if you discover a different method of analyzing a different explanation it might make more sense to you. Doing the study on something fresh helps you to get more knowledge, which will help you figure out which things you need to keep in your mind.

When you genuinely want to ensure something is remembered, consider it and throw it around in your brain a few times. The more you repeat something in your mind, the better you'll learn it and be able to recall it in the future. Using visual aids and even word association can help with your memory too. Utilize a variety of memory assistance available to help improve your memory card.

Chapter 4: Brain Exercises

After discussing mnemonic devices, we move on to the final chapter of this book: a discussion on brain exercises, which are also effective ways to improve one's memory. In chapter 2, it was said that brain exercises are important to constantly keep your brain cells working because dead brain cells will make it difficult to enhance your memory. Thus, this chapter shall provide different brain exercises that you could try on a regular basis.

1.   Memory game – Who would ever forget about the classic memory game? In testing one's memorization skills, this game will come in very handy. Memory games are available online, but you can also create your customized memory game cards. All you have to do is to place similar images on two cards, shuffle these cards, lay these cards face down, and then flip over each card and look for the card with the same image. It is a very simple game, yet it trains our brains to remember where we last saw the card with the same image, thus improving our memorization skills.

2.   Sudoku – Sudoku is a type of logic/brain game puzzle that most people enjoy. To win at Sudoku, you must distribute the numbers 1-9 in 3x3 boxes (contained in a board of many 3x3 boxes) while making sure that each number is unique in its row, column, and particular box.

3.   Riddles – Answering riddles may be tiresome and frustrating, but they are good ways of exercising your brain cells by forcing yourself to think outside the box.

4.   Crossword puzzles – Similar to riddles, answering crossword puzzles is time-consuming, but it is very educational. You are not just exercising your brain, but you are also practicing the art of trying to remember things to answer each item. In this latter part, you may apply the different tips provided in the second chapter for you to remember the answers to each question.

5.   Song lyrics – Song lyrics do not only serve as mnemonics but when used differently, they may also be brain exercises! As a way to test your memorization skills, try memorizing a song every day. The next day, try singing the song you memorized the previous day. Repeat this over and over again, and you will see that memorizing has become easier for you. And who knows? You may also use these memorized song lyrics as your own mnemonic devices!

6.   Attention span exercises – Another way to exercise your brain is to indulge yourself in attention span exercises. This way, you can see how long you can concentrate without getting distracted. As provided in chapter 2, you can opt to try listening to a long lecture and/or read long texts and then list down the things you have picked up in both items to see how much you have recalled and how much you have missed.

7. Name the colors – This is an old brain exercise, but it still works every time. How does "name the colors" work? Simple. You are shown an image where the names of the colors are written – but the colors are written in another color. For example, blue is written in red, red is written in black, and so on. To play "name the colors," you must name the color of the text, and simply not read the name of the color written. Following the previous example, you have to say "red" instead of "blue" because the word "blue" is written in red, etc. This is an excellent exercise to test your focus and your speed in thinking/processing information.

8. 4 pics 1 word – 4 pics 1 word is a modern application available for smartphones, yet it is a very good brain exercise. It works this way: you are given four pictures, and these pictures are connected in one way or another, whether literally or figuratively, and you need to guess the common word that these pictures all lead to given a set of letters and many blocks to fill in. This game will test your recalling skills as well as your association-with-another-memory skills.

9. Spot the difference – Another common and old game is 'spot the difference.' This game may be old, but the effect it has on brain activity is still unfazed. There are plenty of ways to do spot the difference – sometimes you are given only two images to compare, sometimes you are given four. Regardless of the number, your task is to spot the differences in both images.

This trains your brain to work extra hard to spot even the littlest differences, and it enables you to examine things very carefully and with an observant eye.

10.   Name the people in the crowd – If you know that you are not good with remembering names, then this exercise is for you. You can do this exercise in person or using images – either way, and you do it like this: you are in a crowd, or you are looking at a picture of a crowd. Ask someone to name the different people in this crowd, and then give yourself some time. After a while, try reciting the names of the people in this crowd. If you were able to do it the first time, give yourself some time again then try doing it a second time to see if you still remember the names of the people accurately. This will help you improve your name memorization skills, particularly in social gatherings.

There are plenty more brain exercises available on the Internet and/or in puzzle books, but these are just the most common ones that you can use. Remember that an active brain is a healthy brain, and a healthy brain makes memory improvement easier!

Chapter 5: The Making of Memories

There are three main processes involved in human memory: encoding, storage (which includes consolidation), and retrieval. The retrieval process of memory has its roots in the recording process – you can only remember (retrieve) what has become a lasting memory. That means it is important to understand how memories are formed if you want to have a better memory.

There are three stages in the making of every lasting memory of a real-world event. First, we record sensory input into sensory memory. In a matter of seconds, that is moved into short-term memory. Later, that memory is consolidated and moved into long-term memory. It is possible, if we do it right, to go into the farthest reaches of our mind and find much of what has come across our senses. Normally, though, we only remember what we need to remember.

As many have found, writing things down tends to make it easier to recall something later. The aid to memory doesn't come from writing it down so that it is easier to reference the material later on, but comes about because the act of writing, in itself, tells the brain that the material is "important," and needs to be remembered. The brain will then catalog the memory in a way to make recall easier.

Think about some of the clearest memories you have. Are they good ones – or about things that are disturbing? Why is it that you can only seem to remember the things that have had the greatest impact on you and not the things that are inconsequential?

What we remember is, to a large degree, a function of focus. The brain has the potential to record everything, but only earmarks for remembering what we pay attention to. Because what we pay attention to is determined by the impact it has on us, and we remember most readily what has had a significant impact on us.

How we remember something is tainted or intensified by the state, we were in at the time that the memory was created. It affects how long we will remember it, how easily memory can be retrieved, and the ways it can be retrieved.

Later, our state of mind as we retrieve the memory is also important. Memories are subject to interpretation as they are recalled and interacted with. Memories are malleable when they have been retrieved. When memory is returned to "storage," in the process of re-consolidation, that memory will have been changed by the state we were in while the memory was recalled, and by more recent experiences or information. That is one of the reasons why the memories of witnesses in court proceedings must be corroborated – and why a good attorney can change a witness' mind about their memories.

Time is another variable that influences memory. Things change in mind with time, partly due to ongoing changes in the connections between neurons as new data continues to come in, and partly due to changes in the neurochemistry of the brain as we age.

When an event is perceived, it is encoded as a lasting memory in a series of steps. First, the input is interpreted as sensory data in the relevant sensory cortices. For example, when you see something, the visual stimuli are received by the visual cortex, and a memory of the object you saw is created. That memory lasts just long enough – often fractions of a second – as an iconic memory in the visual cortex to provide for continuity of visual data. That slight persistence of the image is necessary for us to make sense of our world, for example, to notice that a specific object in our visual field has moved.

The visual data is then sent on to short-term memory, which is part of the larger organizational construct of working memory (which overlaps both short-term and long-term memory). Attention to the specific sensory stimuli acts like a filter, selecting out what is sent on to short-term memory.

With more filtering for relevance and importance, some memories are sent on from short-term memory to the hippocampus for consolidation with other memories and long-term storage. Each type of sensory data is stored long-term in the sensory cortex that originated it but now marked out by the hippocampus as belonging with memories in other storage locations. In this way, sight, sound, touch, smell, and other memories "know" to activate simultaneously to produce a complete memory when the memory of an "event" is retrieved.

In the process of forming long-term sensory memories, there are three opportunities to forget. If you are overwhelmed with too much visual data coming in and accumulating in the visual cortex before being sent on to the next step in the process, there will be a loss of visual data. This can result in gaps in the memory and mistaken sequences of data being sent from the visual cortex to the hippocampus. That's the first memory glitch.

The second opportunity for memory loss is during the actual transmission of the data between the visual cortex and the hippocampus. That loss of data can be the result of degraded synapses or injury. Aging can play a significant role in both.

The third opportunity to forget arises when the hippocampus attempts to connect the data with the input of other senses. When the data is incorrectly matched up, the logic circuits of the hippocampus are likely to reject that memory. What you end up remembering is a lot of confusion instead of the actual event itself.

When SWAT teams enter a hostile location, such as breaking through the doors of a felon's hideout, they make use of this capacity for the brain to become overwhelmed and confused. They come in fast and hard with smoke bombs and loud explosions (harmless, of course). They do this to overwhelm the senses of the unsuspecting occupant deliberately. In the debilitating confusion that ensues, the officers can swoop in and take control of the situation and anyone in it.

When the hippocampus has too many things coming at it, it trips a cognitive circuit breaker and stops processing. It's a way to keep the conscious part of the brain from grinding to a halt. That results in gaps in memory, or areas where the memory hasn't been strongly encoded, causing rapid degradation of the memory (we call it forgetting), or in incorrect remembering. A simple way to avoid this is to stay underwhelmed. In a world that is going at breakneck speed, it seems almost impossible to slow the information coming at us down, but it is possible.

Short-term memories are those memories stored before being sent to the hippocampus for binding for long-term storage. Although filtered by attention, short-term memories, when they can be retrieved, can be more accurate, not yet having been subjected to the same level of interpretation or bias as occurs with long-term memories. Memories that have been transferred into long-term storage by the hippocampus are not just stitched together and associated with other "relevant" memories, and they are also bound by neurotransmitters, such as dopamine, oxytocin, and epinephrine, which chemically mark and "color" the memory as "good" or "bad."

Individual long-term sensory memories are stored in the sensory cortices from whence they originated after the hippocampus has created connections between them and any related memories. Those connections instruct them to activate simultaneously when retrieved later, forming the total long-term memory.

It takes lots of practice to be able to extract these memories on demand, but it is one of the ways that competitive memory athletes memorize large volumes of data that they then regurgitate accurately. The best way to develop the ability to recall memories from the visual cortex is to train with flashcards. Flashcard training develops the holding capacity of the visual cortex to accommodate larger amounts of visual data, with more robust connections.

Photographic memory

We can't talk about visual memory without talking about "photographic memory."

In popular culture, the term "photographic memory" is used to describe a camera-like, mythic ability to capture almost instantaneously the memory of a picture or an image in exact detail and composition and to recall it as a perfect replica indefinitely, calling it up like a slide that one can study. That sort of ability is just that, a myth, promoted by entertaining movies and books.

However, there is real "photographic memory," which is very useful, although it is not nearly so dramatic as the stories would have you believe. Real photographic memory is simply the ability to remember visual images or information in great detail.

When we think of photographic memory, we are typically thinking of visual memory, stored in the visual cortex. But photographic memory isn't the exclusive domain of the ocular sense. There are five kinds of photographic memories, each emanating from a different sensory cortex, visual, auditory, and so on.

Photographic memory can exist in the same way for the other four senses as well. It is possible to remember the sequence of sound exactly as it was heard. Someone like Beethoven or Mozart could recreate the exact sound of what they had heard, even playing with it in their minds before reproducing the sounds with a musical instrument. That is a type of photographic memory too, only for hearing.

A person can develop photographic memory as it relates to visual events, or a highly accurate sound memory, or accurate memories based on any of the other senses or a combination of senses.

While many people use the phrases "eidetic memory" and

"photographic memory" interchangeably, they are not, in fact, the same thing. Eidetic memory is the ability to capture a faithful mental snapshot of a sensory event after only a few exposures and to recall it vividly with precision without the help of memory devices or mnemonics for some very short time after exposure. Eidetic memory can apply to visual memory or the other senses. Eidetic memory is rare, something you were either born with or you weren't and is believed to be found only in children.

In the end, the difference between a photographic memory and a normal memory is one of degree more than it is of a kind. It is possible to develop the ability to recall more because the human brain is built with the capacity to remember more. However, to conserve energy for survival purposes, the brain only records and recalls events it has reason to believe that we need to remember to survive. That is one of the reasons that we remember things that threaten our existence more than we remember mundane events or objects.

Memory encoding

The process of encoding memories begins when our senses capture the various stimuli we experience. Each sense we have – sight, sound, smell, taste, and touch – captures packets of information and sends that on to the cortex associated with that particular sense.

Specifically, visual information detected by the eyes is sent to the visual cortex. Sound vibrations detected by the ears are sent to the primary auditory cortex. Similarly, touch, smell and taste data are sent to the sensor's corresponding cortex in different parts of the brain.

Those sensory processing regions are located in different areas of the brain for safety. An injury to a specific part of the head might cause a person to lose their eyesight, but their hearing could remain intact because it is in a different part of the brain. Imagine if data from all the senses were processed in the same place. An injury to that spot would render the person without any sensory input whatsoever.

It should be noted that not all types of memories go through the same process. For example, implicit motor memories do not need the hippocampus for their transfer into long-term memory. Those who have had damage to the hippocampus or have had the hippocampus removed can still learn and remember new motor skills even while they are unable to remember how they learned it, and they aren't able to form any other kind of new long-term memory.

All the different types of sensory data arising from an event don't immediately "sync up" in the brain. Sensory data taken in by the sensory organs is transmitted to the relevant cortices at varying times. In particular, light and sound travel at different speeds. Think about that for a second.

Let's say there is an explosion a thousand yards from where you stand. That explosion generates light, sound, heat, tremors, and smell. Each type of data travels at a different speed. Light travels significantly faster than sound. The light from the detonation will be the first thing to reach the observer, so that is detected first by the eyes. The next to arrive is the sound, faster than any prevailing wind could carry the smell of the ignition material. Finally, the tremor underfoot arrives as the vibration takes time to move through hard material.

The various sensory stimuli from one single event arrive at the observer's different sensors at different times and are therefore recorded by each sensory cortex at different times.

The data from the individual channels are then sent to the brain's hippocampus where the different sensory memories are stitched together into one coherent virtual event. But to do that, the hippocampus needs to recognize all these events as the same event, even though they arrived at different times from different sources. So, the hippocampus accounts for that and holds on to the event in a kind of subconscious memory as all the data is brought together and assembled.

Once you have recorded everything into memory, the next question will be whether you can recall them all and in the correct sequence.

Now, for a moment, let's think of a sports photographer as an analogy. A sports photographer has some nifty cameras that can capture hundreds or thousands of frames per second. (The world's fastest camera records over 4 trillion frames per second.) When the photographer is taking pictures of a Formula One race, the event consumes thousands of captures. The shutter release button is pressed, and thousands of images are captured in just a few seconds. Imagine taking pictures just as a car starts to negotiate a hairpin turn until the car pulls out of the turn – how many ever-so-slightly-different images could there be?

Sporting event photographers take their pictures like this for two reasons. First, they are ready for any mishap or unexpected event that may happen, and they won't miss that vital shot. Second, it provides a bank of a thousand images, and they can pick the best of the lot. Out of a thousand captured frames, it is certain that at least one picture will be perfect enough to hang the moment on.

When the photographer returns to the studio, all the images are laid out and scrolled through to find the best one. The rest are dropped into an archive or just deleted if they are irrelevant. Keeping all those unnecessary photos consumes resources. In photography, gigabytes and exabytes of data cost money to maintain in storage.

Like the sports photographer, the senses record thousands of bits of sensory data, thousands of images, for instance. In the brain, storing a unit of memory uses energy, regardless of whether the memory is active or dormant. Just as the photographer goes through the cache of images and chooses what to keep, the brain cycles through the large amounts of data, it accumulates during a day and then encodes for long-term storage the memories it is programmed to keep.

The memory marked out as "important" will get more connections in the brain, while the memory that is not so important will get less. The more neuronal connections the brain makes for a particular memory, the easier the recall process and the longer the memory stays in the conscious recall. Memories that are not considered important are still there, but the synaptic paths to get to them are fewer. Deeper thinking is needed to pull those out of storage gradually.

Now let's take this analogy one step further.

Imagine the same Formula One photographer with thousands of images taken at the event. Going through the image cache for the day, the goal may be to find a particular shot that captured a crash or an image of a particular driver negotiating a bend. Going through the images intent on finding something particular creates a sort of bias. All else is less important when one is found that tallies with that bias, it is chosen.

Our memory operates in the same way. If we have a certain

bias, the memories we keep will be encoded into long-term memory with that bias. We don't just store the raw memory, and we store our interpretation of that memory, an interpretation based on our bias.

So, when we look more closely, we start to see that what appears to be a single event is not the smallest denomination of a memory packet. We see that memory is made up of multiple streams of information stitched together, and that the memory of one event is built one layer at a time from a mosaic of different events.

Those recalled events are virtual, not physical. Think about that for a minute. We get so caught up with reality and our memories of it that we sometimes think that they are the same, or that one is the exact representation of the other. With this, we aren't even talking about confusing fantasy and real events. We are just talking about memory, what we remember. We think of it as "real." It is not. It's not even accurate.

Prior memories dictate how we evaluate newer events, how they are interpreted and stored. This is a process that advances continuously. All this is done in the hippocampus, where memories are stitched together. When we go to sleep at night, those memories are then permanently recorded in a bioelectrical process of creating neurons and pathways.

No memory exists in a vacuum. This is where any attempt to

compare a human memory to a computer hard drive reaches an abrupt limit. While each memory on a hard drive is recorded in a specific address, and that address is recorded in a registry, the human mind places a neuron in the brain and then connects that neuron to a network of other neurons based on their associative value. Every single neuron can have anywhere from a few to several hundred thousand connections: the more connections, the more entrenched the memory. On a computer hard drive, a memory either exists or it does not, whereas, in the human brain, memory exists in degrees.

Chapter 6: How Our Memory Works

Our brain is said to be the most important organ that we have in our body. It controls all the other parts and organs of our body. It also dictates what we should do and what we should not. And of course, our brain is held responsible for all the memories that we form every single day.

Our brain is composed of two types of cells: the neurons and the glia. While the glia is the one who takes the supporting role, it is the neurons that are held responsible for all the mental processes that occur in our brain, such as the formation of memory.

As much as our brain is an important part of our body, our memory is also an essential part of our being. Without our memory, we will not be able to remember the things that we have experienced or retain information. We would have to respond to things as if we did not experience those things at all. We will not be able to recognize even our faces, let alone other people's faces. Without our memory, we would not be able to do practically anything well, or at all.

Three stages of remembering

The process of remembering has three stages. The information that we have acquired has to undergo these stages before it can truly become a memory.

1. Acquisition or encoding. This is the stage wherein your senses acquire the information. For instance, you just met a person and you are told that his name is Luke. That moment you heard the name Luke is the acquisition stage.

2. Storage. This is the stage wherein you store the acquired information in your brain until you need it. For instance, you do not need to think about the name Luke all the time. There are times when you have to think about other things, so you have to store that information in your brain until you need it.

3. Retrieval. This is the stage when you have to retrieve the stored information from your brain because you need it. For instance, you have already stored in your brain that this guy's name is Luke. Therefore, the next time you will get to meet him, you will retrieve the information (i.e., the name Luke) that has already been stored in your brain because you need that information (i.e., you need to call Luke by his name).

If that is too hard for you to remember (because—oh, right!—you have a pretty bad memory), then you can refer to these steps as the "Three R's of Remembering"—Recording (acquisition), Retaining (storing), and Retrieving (retrieval). Just a piece of cake, isn't it?

Two types of memory

There are also two major categories of memory: short-term memory and long-term memory.

• Short-term memory. This refers to the memory that is stored in our brain for a very short time. You either dismiss this memory once you have already used it or you transfer it to the long-term memory.

• Long-term memory. This refers to the memory that is stored in our brain for a longer period. This includes memories that you need for a longer period, thus need to be stored in your brain longer. An example would be the name of your family or your friends. You should not forget this information since it is important to you, so you store it in your long-term memory.

Why we easily forget things

Aside from understanding how our memory works and gets formed, it is also important to understand why we forget this memory easily for us to fight forgetfulness.

You tend to forget things easily—which is probably why you are reading this book. However, you can't just say that you are naturally forgetful, or that you are born that way. Sometimes— or most of the time—things slip out of our mind easily not because of our "natural tendency" to be forgetful but rather because of how we treat these memories.

Researcher Elizabeth Loftus (who is also one of the most celebrated experts when it comes to human memory) once researched as to why we tend to forget things easily. In this research, she has found out four major reasons for our forgetfulness. These reasons include motivated forgetting, interference, failure to store, and retrieval failure.

1.   Retrieval failure. This is perhaps one of the most common reasons as to why we easily forget things. Sometimes we can't retrieve particular information or memory, and we feel like it just vanished out into thin air. One of the possible explanations for retrieval failure is called the decay theory, which states that as new memory is formed in our brain, a memory trace is being created. Through time, this memory trace starts to fade and then disappear. In other words, new memories replace the old ones, which in turn is why it seems hard for us to remember everything. If this memory is not rehearsed and retrieved regularly, then it will be gone eventually.

2.   Interference. This suggests that our memories interfere or compete with each other. It does not necessarily mean that the old memories are the ones that get replaced always; it just means that whenever a new memory resembles an old one, then interference will most likely happen.

There are said to be two types of interference: proactive interference and retroactive interference. The proactive interference is when old memories hinder and make it hard for our brain to acquire new memories, while the retroactive interference is when the new information interferes with the old ones, which makes it difficult for our brain to recall the previously acquired information.

3.   Failure to store. More often than not, we lost information not necessarily because we are just plain forgetful but rather because we were not able to acquire that particular information or that it just never made it to our long-memory in the first place. For example, you may be able to recall the color of the shirt that your friend wore yesterday but not let's say the exact number of circles that are printed on that shirt. That is because the first information—the color of the shirt—made it into your long-term memory while the second one—the exact number of circles printed on the shirt—did not even make it to your brain (perhaps, because you did not pay attention to it at all). And to put this easily: it is just like trying to memorize the entire periodic table when you haven't seen a periodic table yet.

4.   Motivated forgetting. Forgetting is not always accidental. Sometimes, we forget things because we want to, hence the name. Usually, we want to forget those memories that we regard as bad and disturbing such as traumatic experiences or events. It is essentially like deleting unwanted files from your computer.

Other factors that affect our memory

Aside from the reasons of forgetfulness that we have talked about earlier in this chapter, there are still some other factors that also affect our memory. These factors are usually those that have something to do with our lifestyles, such as sleep deprivation, stress, and even bad diet.

1.   Sleep deprivation. At least once in your life, you have probably pulled an all-nighter either as a student. You might think that since you just studied the day or night before your exam, you will be able to remember everything that you have studied (since the memory is still quite fresh in your brain). But more often than not, what happens is the opposite. You forget what you have studied. Why is that so? Because you didn't have enough sleep. As a result, you feel groggy, and your brain somewhat becomes foggy. You also can't focus that much since your brain is feeling tired due to lack of sleep.

Experts also suggest that aside from health problems like obesity, hypertension, and diabetes, sleep also causes impairment in our ability to store memories. That is because as one person sleeps, his brain starts working processing the information that you have acquired from that particular day and begins forming memories. And if you are deprived of sleep, you hinder your brain from processing information and learning as well as retaining new information.

2.   Stress. It is said that when a person gets stressed a lot, there is a higher tendency for him to develop Alzheimer's disease sooner or later in his life. That is because stress can trigger degenerative processes in the human brain, which in turn can lead to memory loss.

Moreover, a study conducted at the University of Iowa has shown that stress can cause an increase in the levels of cortisol—a natural hormone that is produced by adrenal glands—which in turn can lead to lapses in our memory as we age.

"Stress hormones are one mechanism that we believe leads to weathering of the brain," says Psychology Assistant Professor Jason Radley. "Like a rock on the shoreline, after years and years, it will eventually break down and disappear."

3.   Bad diet. The food that you eat may not only affect your body but your brain as well. Experts suggest that eating foods that have high levels of sugar and fat contents can reduce the levels of natural chemicals in our brain, which is said to be harmful to learning and memory. When you eat foods that are rich in sugar and fat, you may be hurting your brain!

A study conducted at the University of California's Brain Injury Research Center, it was found out that eating junk foods—which have high levels of fat and sugar contents—can result to a decrease in the levels of natural chemicals in our brain called Brain-Derived Neurotrophic Factor(BDNF).

BDNF is important in the process of synaptic transmission, in which the brain transforms electrical into chemical impulses for us to remember things. Therefore, if we lack BDNF due to unhealthy diet and eating excessive amounts of junk foods, the responsiveness of our brain during the process of synaptic transmission will be affected. This, in turn, may lead to cognitive decline.

Ten techniques to improve your memory

Now, let us talk about the techniques that you can do to improve your memory! There is no need to worry, though, because these techniques are as easy as saying "I don't remember!"

1.   Pay attention.

Sounds simple right? This is the very first thing that you need to do if you want to improve your memory—pay attention. Lots of attention. If you do not pay attention, then the information will not even make it to the acquisition stage; let alone to the long-term memory! It is just like trying to remember something that you do not even know in the first place.

So if you want to remember something, make sure that you pay attention. For instance, if you want to remember what your boss asked you to do, then listen to what he or she is telling you. Do not think about other things while listening to him or her. Just focus on what he or she is saying so that you will be able to store that information in your brain and retrieve it later when you need it.

2.   Use mnemonic devices.

This is perhaps one of the most effective techniques when it comes to memorization. In mnemonics, you create a pattern that stands for a piece of information that you are trying to remember so that it will be a lot easier for your brain to process.

For example, you are trying to memorize the taxonomic classification, but it is hard for you to remember the kingdom, phylum, class, order, family, genus, and species. With the help of mnemonics, you can assign a pattern to this so that you can easily remember them without actually memorizing them as is. You can say "Kings (Kingdom) Play (Phylum) Cards (Class) On (Order) Fairly (Family) Good (Genus) Settee (Species)." This sentence is a lot easier for you to remember because it makes more sense to you than the original version.

You can be as creative as possible when inventing mnemonics!

3. Create associations.

Association is also a memory device, just like mnemonics. However, an association is more on relating new information to the old ones. For example, if you are bad at remembering names, then you can try associating a person's name with something that is more familiar with you instead of focusing too much on remembering a person's name as is. Let us say that you just met a person whose name is Britney. You can associate her name with say Britney Spears, so that the next time you see her, you will be reminded of Britney Spears, which in turn will make you remember that her name is Britney.

4. Sing.

Do you wonder why it is easier for you to remember song lyrics as compared to the things that are more important than song lyrics? That is because song lyrics come with a tune. The rhythm of a song easily gets stuck in our brain, which is why we easily remember a particular song. Try memorizing the lyrics of a song that you haven't even heard before. It's pretty hard. This is also the reason why there is an ABC song. As a kid, we can't memorize all the 26 letters of the English alphabet. Therefore, they made it into a song so that it will be easier for us to remember.

You can also try doing this on your own. You can either create your tune or sing the things that you are trying to remember to the tune of your favorite song. You will eventually find it a lot easier to recall those pieces of information.

5. Minimize multitasking.

Although multitasking may appear to be helpful, it does not help you make do more things in the long run; let alone remember things. For example, you are trying to study for your geography and chemistry exams. Because you no longer have enough time, you decide to study both of them at the same time (so that you can "save time"). You try to multitask by memorizing names of countries while memorizing elements simultaneously.

That kind of multitasking will not help you in any way possible. Our brain is programmed to process one thing at a time. If you attempt to inject loads of information, the tendency is that your brain will not be able to process all of them, making you forget them. Therefore, instead of trying to remember lots of things at the same time, focus first on one thing and then move on to another once you are done with the first one.

6.   Repeat the information as many times as possible.

If the information is not rehearsed, there is a tendency for it to be overpowered by the new information. As a result, this particular information will eventually disappear from our brain. Therefore, if you want to remember things easily, try to repeat them as many times as possible. Doing so will tell your brain that this information is important, so you need to remember it. Your brain will, in turn, transfer that piece of information from your short-term memory to your long-term memory.

7.   Write things down for better retention.

It is said that writing things down can also help you retain things easily. The process of writing information and reading over it can help you remember the information easily and make sure that you will not eventually forget it. Moreover, you can also easily visualize things if you write them down. Visualizing things can also help you remember easily.

8. Put reminders on places where you can easily see them.

Do you have a lot of things to do yet you keep on forgetting them? Instead of just storing them in your mind, write them down on a piece of paper and post it somewhere so that you can easily see it. For example, if you need to buy some items for tomorrow, you can write down that list of items on a piece of paper and then post that paper on your refrigerator so that when you open your fridge the next day, you will be reminded of the things that you need to buy.

9. Get enough sleep.

As we have discussed in Chapter 1, the lack of sleep can lead to memory loss. Therefore, if you do not want to lose your precious memories, get plenty of rest. Sleep as long as possible so that you will feel energized and not groggy the next day. Do not even attempt to pull an all-nighter the night before your exam because that will not help you. You will only feel tired during your exam day, which will make it hard for you to remember the things that you have studied.

10. Exercise.

Exercise does not only make you stay fit and healthy; it turns out that exercise also makes your memory sharper! In a study conducted at the University of British Columbia, it was found out that engaging in exercise—specifically aerobic exercise— can increase the size of your hippocampus. Hippocampus is a part of the human brain that has something to do with verbal memory and learning.

Moreover, exercise also can lessen insulin resistance as well as inflammation. It also stimulates the production of growth factors in the brain. These growth factors are chemicals that affect the overall health of the brain cells as well as the growth of blood vessels in our brain. Growth factors also affect the profusion and the subsistence of new brain cells.

Generally, exercise also increases the levels of oxygen in our brain. It also lessens the possibility of developing some disorders that can eventually lead to memory loss, like cardiovascular diseases and diabetes.

Chapter 7: Techniques to Improve Your Memory

Memory lapses may be caused by distractions, preoccupation, lack of focus and weak memory muscle. There are numerous techniques to beef up your brain muscles:

Give your brain a workout.

By the time you are an adult, your brain has already formed millions of neural pathways necessary in processing and recalling information quickly, solving easily recognizable problems, and executing common tasks almost instantaneously. But sticking to these timeworn pathways, you deny your brain the stimulation it needs to keep growing and developing. Your brain needs some shaking up from time to time!

The "use it or lose it" principle popular in building muscular strength also applies to memory enhancement. The more you subject your brain to intellectual activities, the better you'll be at remembering information. The best brain exercises take you out of your routine and challenge you to form new brain pathways.

Good brain-boosting activities have the following elements:

• It introduces you to something new. An activity may be

considered intellectually demanding, but if it is something that you've already mastered, then it doesn't qualify as a good brain exercise. The activity needs to be something that you haven't yet tried and is out of your comfort zone. It's your exposure to learning new things and developing new skills that eventually strengthen your brain.

• It's difficult and challenging. The best brain-boosting activities should be hard enough to demand your full attention. But as soon as you've mastered the activity, it won't require as much mental effort anymore and won't challenge you as much as when you were introduced to it for the first time. For example, learning to play a challenging new piece of music on the piano counts. Playing a tough piece, you've already memorized does not.

• It's a skill you can improve on. Search out activities that let you begin at an easy level and move up as your expertise progresses, and your capabilities improve. When a once difficult level starts to feel comfortable, that means it's time to move on to the next level of difficulty.

• It's fulfilling. A sense of fulfillment encourages the brain's learning process. It keeps you engaged and interested. As a result, you are more likely to continue doing it and the greater the rewards you'll reap. So choose activities that, while challenging, are still enjoyable and satisfying.

Think of an activity you've always wanted to try—learning how to play a musical instrument, speaking a foreign language, playing chess, or making pottery. So long as an endeavor keeps you engaged, they are sure to help you improve your memory.

Engage in physical exercise.

Mental exercise is important for brain health, especially when coupled with physical exercise. Physical activities help your brain stay sharp by increasing oxygen supply to your brain and reducing the risks for disorders that affect memory retention such as diabetes and cardiovascular diseases. Exercise also encourages secretion of essential hormones that put stress and depression in check. Perhaps the most important benefit exercise has on the brain is in neuroplasticity, by stimulating new neuronal pathways known to improve memory formation and recall.

Physical Exercises that are Good for the Brain

- Aerobic Exercises

In most cases, aerobic exercises that are good for your heart are good for your brain as well. Here's how cardio exercises benefit your brain.

- Aerobic exercises repair damaged brain cells thereby improving brain function.

- Cardio exercises encourage secretion of the happy hormone

dopamine. This makes you feel relaxed and happier. Regular exercise, in general, alleviates symptoms of depression in people.

• Aim for 120 minutes of moderate cardio exercise each week. You may dedicate an hour swimming in the morning and another hour in the evening for dancing.

• Stick to your exercise plan. Make it a habit and a part of your regular daily routine. It will help if you do it with an exercise buddy so that you could encourage each other.

• Don't push yourself to your limits. An intense exercise wouldn't do more good in decreasing your anxiety levels than an exercise done in moderation. If you are starting, 30 minutes of moderate exercise will already do you wonders.

• Yoga

Yoga, when coupled with meditation, helps focus and calm your mind. It reduces stress and keeps the brain in tip-top shape.

• It's also known to extend your life by slowing down cellular aging.

• People who regularly meditate often say that they feel more positive and that a happy disposition enables them to deal better with daily life challenges.

- Walking

While walking is the simplest and probably the least costly exercise you can do, it is known to improve brain performance greatly.

• Regular walks enable different parts of your brain to communicate with each other. It has something to do with the neural pathways that are strengthened during regular walks. This enhancement of the neural connections makes you better at planning, strategizing, prioritizing, and multi-tasking.

• Also, practically everyone can enjoy a good walk, regardless of their level of fitness or age.

- Jogging or Running

If you are a person with a lot of energy that needs burning, jogging or running are the best forms of exercise you can do at the start of the day.

• A 15-minute run will help reduce that extra energy to a level you need to get through your work for the rest of the day without getting distracted.

• A quick run will also help you bring on a rush of the mood-booster hormone serotonin.

- Group Classes

For motivation and inspiration, consider joining group classes.

You'd always look forward to working out because exercising becomes play more than a boring activity. Plus there's nothing more rewarding than making new friends.

For group activities, you may consider Aqua Zumba, Latin Hip-hop, Family Yoga, Tai Chi, or Group Cycling.

Chew gum while learning new things.

Studies correlate chewing gum with increased heart rate levels resulting in increased circulation of oxygen-bearing blood into the brain. This, in turn, increases activity in the hippocampus, that part of the brain mainly responsible for forming memories.

Move your eyes sideways.

Make this a part of your daily morning exercise. Move your eyes from side to side for 30 seconds. Why? In studies, it was found out that horizontal eye movements strengthen the corpus callosum, a bundle of neuronal fibers that link the brain hemispheres: the creative right brain and the logical left brain.

Clench your fists.

There was a study conducted to determine how body parts may be linked to how the brain functions. It showed that clenching the hands improves a person's ability to memorize things. Making a fist with the right hand aided in learning something, and switching to making a fist with the left helped in the recall.

At first, it seems farfetched that a person's hands have something to do with memory. The explanation given was that the hand-clenching stimulates the brain in a cross-wired manner. Making a fist with your right hand activates the left side of your brain, and the reverse happens with clenching the left hand.

Use unusual fonts.

Funky fonts promote better recall. There was a study that backs up this observation. So if you wonder how making something hard to read makes it easier to remember, here's the explanation: Think of the time you've skimmed through text, got to the end, and then realized that you didn't quite understand what the document said. The study explained that unusual fonts act like speed bumps. Changing the font to make it harder to read will slow you down so you'd read more carefully, consequently improving your recall. A more complex explanation has something to do with confidence. When you encounter writing that's hard to decipher, you become less confident of your ability for comprehension. As you feel nervous about not understanding the material, you concentrate harder and go through it more deeply.

Doodle.

There's nothing like a blank sheet of paper to entice the brain to doodle. Research shows that doodling helps you let loose your imagination. Moreover, creating illegible drawings and writing down random thoughts encourages the brain to improve creative thinking, to stay focused and to retain information.

Laugh.

Laughter helps lower levels of cortisol, the hormone associated with stress. When secreted in high levels, cortisol is known to affect the hippocampus, the short-term memory consolidator, consequently impairing learning and memory.

Humor should be incorporated into your total wellness plan for an excellent quality of life full of memories.

Start with these basics if you are looking for ways to bring more laughter in your life:

• Take yourself less seriously. Share your embarrassing moments and learn to laugh at yourself.

• When you hear laughter, gravitate toward it. You notice that you are always happy to share something funny because sharing feeds off the humor and affords you the chance to laugh again. So if you hear laughter, you knew that you have to seek it out and join in.

• Spend time with playful, fun people. Some people laugh heartily at themselves and the absurdities of life. They are quick to find the humor in everyday situations. Their positive point of view and happy disposition are just contagious.

• Surround yourself with images that light you up. Put up a humorous poster in your office. Set a computer screensaver that never fails to make you smile. Display photos of you and your loved ones having fun.

• Learn from children. Pay attention to children and realize that they are the experts on playing, laughing, and taking life lightly.

Practice good posture.

Posture is often neglected as a conscious expression of one's self. You may not be doing it right, and the good news is it's possible to make improvements on how you hold yourself, how it can ideally shape your life and future accomplishments.

In a series of experiments, it was discovered that body posture could affect the recall of both positive and negative memories. When sitting in a slouch and looking downward, study participants found it much easier to recall helpless and negative memories than empowering and positive ones. When sitting upright with chins up, it's always easy for participants to remember positive memories.

A straight posture generally improves memory because sitting upright encourages increased blood flow and oxygen to the brain by as much as 40 percent.

Feast on the Mediterranean diet.

Researches show that a diet of fruits, vegetables, nuts, and fish (a whole range of food that is common in most Mediterranean fares) is not only good for your heart but your brain as well. Vegetables and nuts are likely to fend off memory loss especially in late adulthood. Fruits and Omega-3 in fish are anti-oxidants that will protect you from cognitive decline.

Take caffeine-rich drinks to enhance your memory consolidation.

Whether it's a cup of tea, a can of soda or a mug of freshly brewed coffee, consumption of caffeine is the chosen energy booster for people who want to wake up or stay up. Studies have found another use for this stimulant: memory enhancer. Although most of these studies found that caffeine has little effect in creating new memories, the substance has improved memory recall. Research has identified caffeine to be a major player in memory consolidation, a process where memories created were strengthened leading to a deeper level of memory retention and that therefore the substance is better ingested after learning a task.

Be careful, though, to check if caffeine seems to interfere with your sleep at night. If it does, reduce intake or cut it off altogether.

Meditate to improve your working memory.

The working memory could be likened to a chalkboard, where you temporarily "write" bits of information like the location details of a place you are visiting for the first time or names and faces of people you meet in an event. You hang on to these chunks of data until you are ready to sort them into those that you let go entirely (because you have no use for them anymore) or those that you commit to long-term memory (for later recall and use).

Working memory is the same place where you do quick mental computations and hold random details when engaged in conversation.

How does meditation help strengthen the working memory? Studies show that regular meditation enhances your ability to focus. Meditation will enable you to have more control over your alpha rhythm when your brain experiences small smooth bursts of electricity sending you into a state of complete relaxation. This not only improves your creativity but it enables you to filter out all distractions making it easy for you to store important things to memory.

Have a good night's sleep.

Sleep is an important factor in memory storage. It is during slow-wave sleep that the hippocampus replays all the events that happened during your waking moments. Working under compressed time, it sorts through your experiences as it files away those which are relevant while discarding those that won't be significant in the future.

Cultivate a good sleeping habit by doing the following:

• Commit to a regular sleep schedule by going to bed at the same time every night and getting up at the same time every morning. Don't break your routine, even on weekends and holidays.

• Avoid TVs, phones, computers, and tablets an hour before bed. The blue light emitted by these gadgets triggers wakefulness by suppressing secretion of melatonin that induces sleepiness.

If you suspect that caffeine keeps you up at bedtime, reduce your intake or cut it out entirely. Some people are overly sensitive to caffeine that even coffee taken in the morning interferes with sleep at night.

Pay attention.

Do you remember that time when you were planning to buy a red Chevrolet, and suddenly you noticed that what catches your attention during your daily commute are all the red cars plying your route? Pieces of information are committed to your memory because you are interested in them. When you develop a fascination for things around you, you automatically observe important details and get them laser-etched on your brain.

Make time for friends.

Research shows that maintaining worthwhile friendships and a support system are vital not only to mental and emotional health but to brain health as well. In a study conducted by the Harvard School of Public Health, researchers discovered that individuals with active social lives had the slowest rate of memory decline.

There are ways you could take advantage of the memory-boosting benefits of socializing, such as volunteering, joining a club, or reaching out to someone over the phone.

Concentrate.

There are no fast-charging shortcuts to increase your concentration. Today's world is so full of distractions; not to mention the huge volume of information that we need to process every day. We cannot sort through all the information we are bombarded with day in and day out. Then there's the challenge of determining what information to keep and how to recall them fast. The secret here is to tackle big issues first so your brain won't be pre-occupied with matters that may unnecessarily clutter available brain storage space.

Use Mnemonics.

Another effective tool in memorization is called mnemonics. A mnemonics is a tool (a rhyme, an acronym, an image, or a phrase) to help you remember facts or large amounts of information.

There are different types of mnemonic devices, namely:

• Visual image. The trick is to associate a word or a name with a visual image that is colorful, vivid, and three-dimensional. Example: To remember the name Robert Goldman, who works as an inspirational speaker, you may conjure an image that you can associate with him, like a golden robot (which sounds like Robert) that is talking non-stop (his work involves speaking.)

• Acrostic. Create a sentence where the first letter of each word represents the initial of what it is you want to remember. Example: "My Very Excited Mother Just Served Us Nine Pies" where the first letter of each word is the first letter of the planets in our Solar System in order (Mercury, Venus, Earth, Mars, Jupiter, Saturn, Uranus, Neptune, and Pluto); or if without Pluto: "My Very Educated Mother Just Served Us Noodles."

• Acronym. An acronym is a word formed to represent the first letters of all the words that make up a group of keywords or ideas. Example: The acronym "HOMES" will help you recall the names of the Great Lakes: Huron, Ontario, Michigan, Erie, and Superior.

• Rhymes. Rhymes are effective ways to remember more common facts and figures. Example: To remember which months have 30 days and which ones have 31, the following rhyme is helpful: "30 days hath September, April, June, and November. 28 days makes February fine, but in a leap year, it has 29.

• Chunking. Chunking is breaking up a series of characters or a long list of numbers into more manageable, easy to remember portions. Example: Breaking a 10-digit number (say 5558765903) into three sets of numbers (555-876-5903) makes memorizing it a lot easier.

• Method of loci. Also known as the memory palace, memory journey, or mind palace technique, this mnemonic device works by imagining placing items you want to remember along with a familiar route or specific places in a familiar building (or "palace") or room. Example: For a shopping list, picture a puddle of milk in the entryway to your house, eggs sitting on the sofa, slices of bread scattered up the stairs, and bananas on your bed.

Sing.

Music is not only an excellent mood enhancer but a good memory tool as well. Singing exercises the right side of the brain. Consequently, it makes you perform better at problem-solving. Ever notice how you can easily rhyme words when you are singing them than when you are speaking them? This is because the song's melody has activated the pattern recognition ability of the right side of your brain.

Stay Curious.

Always have a good appetite for learning new things and an unquenchable thirst for new knowledge. This is one of the most effective pieces of advice you can get to keep your brain in tiptop shape. Learning a new concept now and then heightens your awareness. Consequently, heightened awareness leads to understanding. Everything you understood, you'd easily remember. For example, knowing that the value of pi is the ratio between the circumference of a circle and its diameter, you are sure that it is a constant value because no matter the size of the circle, it is always the same shape. Interestingly, the value of pi is an irrational number that goes on and on. But you can memorize the first 7 digits of pi by remembering this sentence: "How I wish I could calculate pi." Count the number of letters in each word. It will give you 3.141592.

Read.

We can also gauge the memory power of a person by the size of his vocabulary. Effective speakers will tell you that they do it by reading as much as they can devour. If you don't have the luxury of time, you may build your vocabulary by learning one word each day. To reinforce commitment to memory, use your word-of-the-day at every opportunity by using it in your interactions. That is easily 365 words a year, more than enough words to make a good impression during conversations.

Chapter 8: The Memory Graph

What is the memory graph?

Every individual possesses an episodic memory that stores daily experiences such as visiting various locations, having conversations with people, meeting people and basically a track down of all our activities.

Even in Artificial Intelligence the intelligence agent requires a memory to store experiences, information, and knowledge about the world at large and themselves. Similarly, a person's knowledge/perception of the world or their meaning of a specific conversation is accumulated within the semantic memory.

What differentiates memory graph from other artificial intelligence systems is that it is an integrated mechanism of both semantic and episodic memory based on the construct that creates a unified acyclic graph. Memory graph combines with an external knowledge database. Memory Graph is compatible with tiny footprints that run on Android devices appropriate for mobile applications and other devices.

When it comes to long-term, Memory Graph can be scaled to the vast human data amount based on the data framework Apache Spark.

All our everyday life information is broken into episodic or semantic parts. It is split into fundamental units or organized information through a nodal network or a graphics data structure.

Memory Graph is capable of capturing and storing various types of information such as

Conversations between humans and artificial intelligence agents or contextual metadata related to conversations. It also includes all the reasoning and other conclusions that are done by agents to process brain input and create responses during conversations. Intelligence agents may transfer and swap information and other types of knowledge transferring either a part of or the entire Memory Graph within each other. In future, a memory transfer can be possible between an artificial intelligence agent and a human user.

Do you know how your program data appears? Memory graphs demonstrate the memory power of a specific program. It is made up of vertices that represent memory content or edges for potential access paths. Memory graphs are involuntarily captured for making data structures more accessible. All common data structures are efficiently represented on the graph.

A Memory Graph unified, all-encompassing and integrated representation of both the semantic and episodic relies on a triple construct that uses a combination of a dedicated acyclic graph. It unifies with external knowledge platforms to support short and long-term memory with tiny footprints that run on compatible devices. Long-term Memory Graph is completely scalable to include human level data amount relying on the Big Data Apache or Spark framework.

Foundations For Better Learning

Our learning begins primarily in school. However, paradoxically, we don't learn very effectively in school. School learning methods primarily rely on memorization or learning through rote methods that may be effective for short or arbitrary tests but not when it comes to long-term learning. We may not absorb the concept or essence of learning in our zest for mugging up information. Absorbing learned material is the key when it comes to learning techniques. Here is a list of some pointers for making your learning even more effective and power-packed.

Practice makes a man perfect

This is a no-brainer yet practice testing has been identified as one of the most efficient learning methods by memory and learning experts. It is great from the perspective of not just recalling information from short-term memory but also retaining important bits of information. Practice testing has more than a century of research to boot for its efficacy as a learning technique. You don't have to test yourself in a specific environment.

Self-testing can be done anytime or anywhere by posing questions to yourself and coming up with answers. Use flash cards for testing. Solve problems with notes or text material. You can also put yourself for testing in a test environment.

Why does testing work so effectively? It boosts your retention powers by stimulating complicated processes by gaining access to the long-term memory periodically. It also tests your facilities by encoding more efficient mediators through targets and clues. Recent evidence in the field of learning research suggests that practice also enhances the learner's ability to organize knowledge, thus increasing the efficacy and speed of the retrieval process.

Distributed practice

Distributed practice is a method through which a person's studies are spread out over specific time intervals over a single large work chunk. This is precisely why mugging up for a test doesn't ensure better absorption, learning, and retention. The primary reason distributed practice is so effective is because it offers the brain more time for absorbing information by alternating between both diffused and focused thinking mode. There is sufficient evidence pointing to the fact that spacing out studies facilitates better absorption and retention of information.

AA 1979 study revealed that students who spread out their learning into 6 study session at regular intervals throughout a month between consecutive lessons did their best when it came to a test a month after the final 6th learning session.

Although it would be great if you were awarded 30 days between study sessions, you may not have that much time in an ideal world. Generally, classes go on between 3 to 4 months and feature around 2-4 extensive tests during the entire phase. In such a scenario, use a 24 hour spacing period for restudying the material.

Within the first few learning days, the learning can be spaced out between a 24 hour period between every review. The review sessions can be further broken down into broader lessons. Let a month pass after the initial review sessions. Distributed practice, as well as practice testing, skyrocket your test scores. The ideal scenario is combining practice testing and distributed practice for most effective retention.

Self-Explanation

Self-explanation is closely related to elaborative interrogation. Using this method, an individual explains or records how they conclude. This is a popular technique for resolving general problems. The technique is more effective when it happens during the initial stages of learning. The learning strategy can be used for a wide variety of subjects and tasks. Studies reveal that the method does need greater training and can be one of the most time-consuming study methods. There have been multiple study methods tested for long-term retention through self-explanation.

While practicing self-explanation, participants write down questions they want to ask themselves and later mention the answers. The act of writing down questions and answers helps your memory absorb the concept, and allows the brain to organize materials.

Interleaved practice

The interleaved practice involves students studying topics that blend both the current concept and related concepts studied earlier or during the same time. For example, if a student is learning Algebra polynomials currently, they may want to combine it with previous concepts of algebraic equations or solving inequalities learned during previous weeks.

Interleaved practice implies students should spend a majority of their time studying the current topic at hand, but it should also involve previously studied concepts such as algebraic equations and inequality sums.

Mind Mapping and Creative Thinking

Mind mapping is one the most effective ways of capturing your thoughts and getting them to life in a more visual format for better retention. It goes beyond taking notes. Mind maps help an individual get more creative, retain more information and increase problem-solving abilities. Here's everything you need to know about the powerful mind mapping technique.

What exactly are mind maps?

Mind maps are essentially visual diagrams that link information to the main topic. Think of it as a tree (as the main theme or topic) with branches or sub-branches having ideas woven around the central theme or topic. For instance, let us say your main topic is English literature. The branches (subtopics) can be closely related ideas like types of writings or genres of English literature, eminent English literature authors, publications or books that defined English literature and other similar subtopics. The branches are all closely linked to one another.

Mind maps can be utilized for anything from learning a new language to developing more positive habits. Use an application for creating a knowledge bank through which you can attach files and links, establish goals, write book summaries and solve problems.

How does mind mapping score over long notes or several other brainstorming techniques?

Here are some reasons why mind maps can be one of the most

effective note-taking or brainstorming techniques.

Mind mapping is a graphical tool that involves words, phrases, numerical, visuals and colors, which makes it more enjoyable to make and keep reviewing. The combination of verbal and visual aids makes it six times more efficient when it comes to retaining and recalling information that only words. Visuals used in mind maps back-up words to facilitate better retention. Mind maps connect a group of ideas by establishing a natural link between them to create even more ideas, offers prompt for filling more matter or finding a deeper meaning to the given subject.

You can create ideas fast with the technique or encourage the creation of several creative neural pathways. Mind maps are proven to be effective when it comes to accumulating a high amount of information, and getting an overview of the same.

The technique is especially helpful if you are stuck for ideas or facing a writer's block. You start by creating a starter concept and then follow it up with basic questions such as how who, why or what, etc. One follows each subtopic as it further covers an aspect of the main topic, and expands into several other sub-sub topics to create a more fleshed out version. Once you begin penning ideas using the highly visual mind map, ideas will flow effortlessly. The technique works owing to the powerful principle of association.

Another advantage of the mind mapping technique is that is an easy to access and intuitive and effective way of organizing thoughts owing to the fact mind maps mimic the manner in which information is stored in our brains. Humans don't engage in lateral thinking. Our brains are constantly bouncing ideas.

Let us assume you have to think of different ways to use a stone, you may think of normal uses such as putting them on pathways or rock gardens. Then by getting an overview of its properties, you can think of other less common uses such as a using it as a paperweight, a heavy stone as an exercise and workout routine – you see where this is going? One thing leads to another, and there are endless possibilities.

Making mind maps

Mind maps can be created on paper, using a drawing application on the tablet or using a mind mapping software too. Use channels that facilitate comfortable and effortless usage. Using a pen and paper may be more effective when it comes to gathering your thoughts quickly and effectively by drawing branches and facilitating recollection of details.

Utilizing computer programs can make mind maps even more searchable, which also allowing you the flexibility of including attachments. Look for an application that allows you to add links, include attachments, file notes, export to additional programs, filter content and use key shortcuts.

Once you've identified a tool, here is a step by step process for creating a mind map as described by Tony Buzan, the British author who has patented and trademarked the "mind map" term in the 1960s.

1. Begin at the center of each blank page and then turn it sideways. Starting in the middle of the page will offer your brain the freedom to go in multiple directions for expressing its thoughts in an effortless, natural and unrestrained manner.

2. Use visual or image around the central idea. For instance, if you are writing a Sci-Fi book, you may want to have an image with your main characters or the main plot/theme at the center of the page. The key image will trigger more interesting and stimulating ideas that keep your brain focused while giving it a much-required buzz for coming up with more fleshed out ideas.

3. Use colors generously while creating mind maps. Colors stimulate and excite the brain pretty much like visuals. They add greater depth and vibrancy to your Mind Map while giving the much-needed impetus to your creative energy and making the process of idea generation more fun rather than taxing.

4. Link the main branches to the primary image and connect it to the level 2 and 3 branches. The brain works through association by closing linking or clustering a few things

together. When you link these branches, you may understand or recall information more efficiently and effortlessly. The branches should be curved and not linear. This is because the brain doesn't find straight lines exciting, which may not make it conducive for learning or retention.

Use a single keyword in each line because standalone keywords give your Mind Map greater power and flexibility. Use visuals throughout the mind maps since each picture or image like the main image represents several words. Each picture equals a thousand words, which means if you have 12 visuals or images within the Mind Map, you already have data worth 12,000 words. Now 12,000 words of notes aren't so bad.

The most important thing about a Mind Map is the fact that there are no fixed rules for creating it. You have the flexibility to use it in a way that works for you. You can add more than a single keyword if you find it easier to remember. Mind Maps are highly personal learning and memorization rules, which are about using techniques that work for you.

Faster and More Efficient Learning Introduction To Memory Techniques

Whether you are a student, a parent or a professional, training your memory is the key to getting things done. It could be used for anything from learning a new language to picking up a new skill (such as driving, learning to swim or learning to play the guitar) to addressing a large audience. Picking up new skills can be demanding and time-consuming. However, science can help you speed things up a bit. Here are some fast and efficient learning and memory techniques.

Exercise

Working out is a great way for the body and brain to reap rich benefits. Increased physical activity is known to boost memory, learning, and retention. If you are falling short of ideas or can't get yourself to solve a problem, try going for a walk or slipping into a quick gym session.

Relate new information to existing information

According to research conducted by the Loma Linda University School of Medicine, an amazing technique for memory retention is to connect new information with what is already known. For instance, if you are learning more about Shakespeare's classic Hamlet, you may associate it with other works or tragedies of Shakespeare, the historical era in which he lived and other related facts. This will help you learn and retain information more effectively.

Teach other people what you have just learned

Share your brand new learning or knowledge with someone if you want to strengthen the learning process. The process through which you convert information within the brain into your own words and expressions reinforces the information within the brain. There are several innovative methods to break down concepts into easy to understand bits, which is beneficial for everyone.

There is also another powerful, quick and effective learning technique. When you say something aloud, the brain registers it through auditory signals, thus imprinting the information even more effective within the brain.

Rely on Mnemonics

Mnemonics are a simple yet effective technique for remembering words or phrases that are otherwise challenging to memorize. It is especially useful when it comes to long lists. All of us have used "My Very Educated Mother Just Served Us Nine Pizzas" where each letter of the sentence stands for the first letter of the planet. Music is a potent mnemonic for offering structure and information through repetition. Isn't it easier to retain a catchy tune than a bunch of boring letters such your password? This is precisely the reason advertisers utilize jingles for allowing the message to stay in your mind firmly. We've learned the alphabet most effectively using the alphabet song. There is a Fifty Nifty song for memorizing the 50 states of the USA. You can memorize item lists using the peg system or hook system for every number.

Using the peg system, you utilize a visual that rhymes with the number. Each image or visual of image offers a hook to remember things, mainly in a sequence. Let us say you have a grocery list with items such as one=gun two=loo, three=tree, four=door and so on.

Create a vivid mental visual of the rhyming item for each object. How does a bun look? What kind of a loo is it? How does the tree look? How does the door look? Now create a downright hilarious story in a sequence around the items as we did with the palace earlier. His will make committing the list to memory easier. It will take imagination, effort, and creativity to memorize the list. However, you are likely to retain the information more effectively than simply memorizing through words. Once the main rhyming peg is done, you can use it every time you want to remember the same list.

Make brand new visual links

It is absurd that our memory retains most effectively. Visualization is a critical factor. Tangible objects are easier to remember because they have a clear form that the mind can retain. However, names and numerical information is abstract, and it isn't easy to latch on these vague concepts. The human brain finds it easier to retain clear and tangible images.

Take for instance a person's name is Mike. You will have to associate it the name with something so that the information is stored beyond the short-term memory. Using a series of visual techniques, you can connect Mike to a tangible object such as a microphone. If it is a multi-syllable name such as Melanie, you can think of a melon plus knee. Better still, link the two and think of a melon squashing a knee.

Another way is to use distinctive features of the person and link it with detailed visuals that will make it easier for you to remember. For instance, Mike may have a large nose so you can visualize a microphone with a massive nose or a microphone coming out of his nostrils.

Try and involve as many sense organs as possible for remembering abstract information. The more senses you involve, the better will be your memory's capacity for retaining information. Play into your sense of taste, smell, sight, hearing, etc. when you attempt to remember things. For instance, in the example of Melanie, you can imagine juice squeezing out of the watermelon using your sense of smell (how does the melon smell?) and visual (the sight of squeezing melon).

Write instead of typing

You are likelier to remember more effectively when you write notes by hand instead of typing them. The physical task of writing is known to stimulate particular cells located at the base of our brains known as the reticular activating system or RAS. When the reticular activating is stimulated, the brain devotes greater attention or awareness of your current activity.

When you write with your hand, the brain is increasingly active in constructing every letter.

Studies have pointed to the fact that when notes are taken mechanically through a laptop, the lectures are transcribed in a more verbatim fashion by the brain. However, when notes are hand-written, we tend to transcribe them using our verbal expressions, thus facilitating learning. It merges visual aspects and written words for our brains to latch on.

8 The Art of Remembering Everything

There are several hacks for remembering information such as names, numbers, shopping lists, telephone numbers, historical facts and more. These are smart tricks and tips for programming the brain to remember things more effectively. The innovative methods help you imprint the information firmly into the long-term memory. Here are some smart ways to remember everything from appointments errands to tricky numbers to dates and more.

Remembering numbers

Numbers are tough to remember. Unlike words or verbal information, numbers are more complex and abstract. You will most likely not remember the zip code of your last three homes. You may have to look up your pin numbers or numerical passwords each time you want to complete a transaction. Here are some of the best tips for retaining everything from pin number to debit card numbers.

Numerical memories are already formed in our mind. The key to remembering new information is to associate it with numerical information that already exists. Build connections with already existing digital memory to remember new numbers more effectively. If you are finding it challenging to come up with an association using a particular number, move to the next number in the series and try to come up with an association using it.

Breaking big numbers into smaller chunks makes it easier to memorize them. A regular person can remember only seven random digits as a unit of information within the capacity of their memory. However, through chunking or organizing the data/information into bits, there is a higher chance of increasing the brain's capacity to retain information. This is why phone numbers are broken into clusters of three digits. Try memorizing a number such as 809678541. If you attempt to memorize it as a 10 digit number, you'll have a tough time. However, if you identify them as two separate dates strung together (8/09/67 and 8/5/41), your chances of retaining the information will significantly increase.

Our short terms memory can only store a certain amount of information such as a maximum of seven items. The chunking method helps to overcome this limitation.

Look for establishing a pattern even if it isn't obvious. Look for an association or relationship between numbers. Does the first and second number add to create the third and fourth number? Is there a clear sequence of odd and even digits? Use the available information for creating stories with random numbers. For example, I had a credit limit of $5,700, and once that's exhausted, I am beginning at zero and building it right back up a dollar at a time for remembering a number like 5700 1234. You are creating a story that is hard to forget using numbers to make the retention more power-packed.

Repetition is the key to learning new information and numbers are no different. Once you memorize a large number, use a timer to think about it and make connections with it less than an hour after you've come across the number. According to research, our memory is most susceptible to forgetting information within an hour of acquiring it. It can be misinterpreted or degraded in several ways if not committed to long-term memory. Repeat numbers after 24 hours, followed by a week, and then finally a month. The objective is to repeat information until you remember it.

Memorizing dates

Create vibrant visuals linked with the date you want to remember. The more absurd and strange the connections, the easier it will be to recall the date.

Another effective way of memorizing dates is to learn to organize the information in a more meaningful and systematic manner. It is tough to commit to memory information that is unorganized or not in any clear sequence. Look for several ways to classify dates, so they are easier to memorize.

Make a timeline of dates to relate them to one another and establish logical connections. The more they are put into a context, the more meaningful they become. For example, if you are learning the birthdates of family members, map it into a family tree so you can visually recall the dates as you mentally climb this tree.

Associate numbers with letters to remember dates more effectively. Follow this key to make the dates more memorable. 0= Z (since zero begins z), 1= T (since numerical T and number 1 are written with a single stroke), 2=N (when rotated, the letter resembles 2), 3= M (when it is rotated, the letter resembles number 3), 4=R (the number 4 resembles backward R) and also ends with "R", 5= L (since L is the Roman number for 50), 6=G (since the number 6 and letter G look similar), 7= K (since K rotated clockwise resembles 7's mirror image), 8=B (the number 8 and B look similar) and 9= P (since they are a mirror image of each other).

Use flashcards to memorize facts and information. You can either use a regular set of cards or an electronic application. Write a date on one side of the card and the event on the other.

Shuffle cards and look at the date on every card. Recall the significance of each date. Similarly, start with the event or significance of the date, and check if you can recall the date from memory.

The way it works for many people is, once they remember specific dates, they put away those cards and focus on learning dates that they have trouble remembering. Use flashcards periodically but work only for a few minutes each day. Don't try to cram too much information at a time since it won't be too effective.

Keep repeating the dates to make memorizing it more effectual. We lose vital information within a day of memorizing it, which means it has to be committed to memory immediately. If you keep repeating the information, it will increase memory power and retention. Continue memorizing the information for thirty days to increase your chances of remembering it for several years. Go over a bunch of dates periodically if you are studying for an exam since review makes your learning even more power-packed.

Learning new words

One of the best ways to learn new words is to understand its application. The brain will remember it more effective only when it is used. For example, you've heard a new word, and you know how to use it. However, the brain doesn't recall or remember the word for the future. The best way to get the brain to remember it is by memorizing it. Make ten sentences using the word you desire to learn.

If it has a verb, try using different tenses. By constructing sentences, you are increasing your brain activity and getting it actively involved in the learning and memorizing process.

Record yourself in your voice while saying the words aloud. Feel your mouth moving, while you make connections within the brain. The words need to be associated with the sound for your brain to make the connection. Use a mobile camera or phone to record yourself speaking the new words, and using them in sentences.

Use images to link words to their meanings visually. Even though it sounds absurd, the trick works wonders. The brain has information pouring in every moment that it is challenging to retain information unless we bring in the novelty factor. Make a funny image that depicts the word meaning to enable the brain to pick it up faster.

If you are trying to learn too many words, string them all together into a tall tale that's downright hilarious. Make an insane story using all the words since stories are easier to recall and remember. Picture the story in your mind using details. Repeat the story using the bunch of new words or attempt to connect it in hilarious ways.

Recycle words using prefixes, suffixes, roots and more. For example, you may not remember microbiology, but it is easy to remember micro and logy, which means the study of something tiny (micro means small, and logy means science). We know that logy means the study of something and micro means tiny. Using prefixes, suffixes, and roots, it is easier to string together words for better memorization and recollection.

Memorizing speeches

Memorizing speeches soon is not an easy task. However, using a few hacks and tried and tested strategies, it is possible not just to learn the speech but also have fun doing it. The key is practice, fun, and repetition.

Take paper and pen, and draft the entire speech. If the speech is short, write it down several times. Some people find greater success recording information actively. Writing the speech and recording will help you commit it to memory more efficiently.

Divide a long speech into multiple bullet points. Break up the speech into themes of paragraphs to make retention easier. Don't aim to learn the speech word by word. Rather break it up into several paragraphs with a clear objective for each. For example, start with introduction, body, and conclusion.

Within the body of the speech too, divide the matter into points so each point becomes a paragraph on which you can later elaborate. This will help you add more natural elements than mugging the entire speech mechanically.

Create a list of topics that you are most petrified about. Then, attempt to cover those fears by using memorization techniques mentioned throughout the book such as memory palace. Use deep breathing exercises to calm your spirit when you forget everything.

At times, you may believe that you know what you want to say but when it comes to delivering the speech. However, practice the speech before a bunch of trusted people. Ask friends for tips to do well. Let them be the audience, and tell you if you are audible.

6 powerful tips to help you remember just about anything

1. The most awkward situation is when our memory fails us when it comes to memorizing names. However, you can make the retention more effective by establishing a link between the abstract name and person. It may take some effort. Ask the person you've just met some question.

This will give you the time to repeat their name mentally. Then, introduce them to another person by repeating their name (now you've mentally gone over the name and repeated it aloud too). Make eye contact, say the person's name and make a visual hook for the person's name with their face.

2. Use the power of music for memorizing information and learning more effective. We will forget long speeches and answers but seldom lyrics of songs we like. Music helps us commit information to memory through rhythm, music, and alliteration. This is especially helpful when it comes to learning a foreign language. Train with music, subtitles, and Karaoke.

3. Use your auditory power for remembering information rather than merely reading it. Wasn't your learning more effective when you listened to your teacher rather than reading what's in the book? When you play a song while studying, you will be able to recall the information more effectively by replaying the tune in your mind. People who learn efficiently using this method are strongly attracted to auditory learning. Try recording your lectures and hearing them back over and over each time you are driving or while studying.

4. If you need to remember regularly, such as going taking medicines at a specific time, there are several ways to make it easier to remember. Write a note and place it where you can easily view it. Exposing yourself to the message can make remembering and recalling things easier. Write the message in a region where you can see it such as a screen, refrigerator, computer, and bathroom mirror. Keep feeding or imprinting the message in your brain to make memorization more impactful.

5. Elaborate on your knowledge and learn to focus on new knowledge by associating it with existing knowledge. You may not remember what you wore last Monday for work, but you won't forget what you wore for a special occasion such as a prom. New information is powerfully encoded when it is related to already existing information. You are assigning new information to what you know. The more rational connections you can establish, the more effective it is for committing new information to memory.

Learning or memorization is not a fixed activity. The brain is constantly establishing new connections information you know and what you are currently learning. Compare existing information to cement new information.

6. It is more effective to cover what you like over a longer period than trying to pack everything into the brain in a single sitting. Your brain has a limited capacity when it comes to learning new information at one time. Notice how repeatedly going over what you need to memorize over time rather than mugging can make your learning more effective.

Students try to cram everything into their brain in a single sitting, which makes learning a vast amount of information near impossible. It isn't that if you study at the last moment just before an examination, you won't remember information while writing the examination. You may recall everything for the examination, but the memory may not last long.

Chapter 9: Meditation Techniques For Memory Improvement

Another way you can improve your memory is through meditation. This chapter will teach you basic meditation techniques that should help you find calm, peace, and greatly improve your memory.

What is meditation?

Simply put, meditation is an ancient practice that is often related to religious and spiritual needs. It is the art of staying still and silent and achieving inner peace as well as a better understanding of yourself and your surroundings.

Meditation and Memory

Recent medical studies have shown that meditation is not only beneficial for those who want to relieve themselves of stress or achieve mental calm. Regular meditation also affects the brain in a positive way. It thickens the cerebral cortex or the part of the brain associated with memory, and other basic mental functions. Therefore, it can be safely concluded that meditation helps keep the brain sharp, and will certainly have a good effect on your memory.

Two Basic Meditation Techniques

1. Concentration Meditation

This is the simplest kind of meditation technique as it only requires you to focus on a certain sound until you experience a calm mental wash over you. You can play soothing music, sit in an upright position, and take deep breaths, all the while concentrating on the pattern of the song. This kind of meditation is a great stress reliever, and it also keeps your memory sharp because you are training your mind to pay greater attention to patterns and sounds.

2. Mindfulness Meditation

Mindfulness meditation involves being completely at peace, but entirely aware of your immediate surroundings and the thoughts you are entertaining. This is usually the kind of meditation we see in movies, where the individual is sitting cross-legged in an open field, or a quiet pocket in the forest. The individual looks as if he is asleep, but in actuality, he is sharpening his senses, and allowing his mind to notice the small details that he once took for granted.

Increasing Your Self Confidence In Your Memory Abilities Through Neuroplasticity

Of course, all the memory capacity in the world would be useless if you aren't confident enough in your abilities to commit things to memory and then recall them as soon as you need to do so. A lot of people who have extraordinary memory capabilities are defeated by those who only have an average level of memory simply because the former was too scared, too doubtful of his abilities. This chapter will show you how you can achieve a sense of self-confidence with regards to your memory through the application of neuroplasticity techniques.

What is neuroplasticity?

People who engage in neuroplasticity techniques believe that you can shape or sculpt your brain for better or worse. This means that aside from the inborn intelligence we have upon birth, we are also gifted with the ability to increase or decrease our brain power depending on how we handle and react to different experiences. Thus, neuroplasticity is the term used to describe how malleable the brain is, and how responsive it is to our beliefs and emotions.

Build your self-awareness to increase your self-confidence.

At its core, neuroplasticity is all about increasing an individual's level of self-awareness. Being conscious of how you think, how you speak and how you feel allows you to make constructive criticisms and critical decisions by becoming a detached observer of yourself. For example, you find yourself in a spelling quiz contest, and the stakes are high as you are in the running to become the overall champion. It is the last question, and suddenly you become afraid that you will forget all the words you memorized. The effect is immediate. Once you hear the word to be spelled, you experience mental-block. You struggle to remember the spelling and try in vain to come up with the correct answer. Your opponent smugly writes the word on his board. He wins the championship.

Most people will punish or berate themselves for forgetting something so important. They will focus on the fact that they lost, and the fact that they suddenly forgot what they had studied so long to remember. They will tell themselves repeatedly how they could have won if they did not suddenly experience mental-block. Unconsciously, they decrease their self-confidence.

On the other hand, people who are aware of the brain's malleability will take a step back from the situation, and observe as objectively as possible, the cause of the untimely loss. These people will realize that they were nervous as soon as the quizmaster began talking. They will see themselves lose focus and concentration, and they will understand that what happened was normal and that anyone could have experienced the same thing. They will also learn that the mistake was an innocent one, but something they could have prevented nonetheless.

This heightened awareness of the self is just what they need to improve their self-confidence. Next time, they will no longer give in to the pull of nervousness, knowing full well that the source of nervousness wasn't the opponent or the quizmaster, but the self. As they practice and get better at spelling, they will commit these happy experiences to memory, and draw on those as a source of strength and confidence.

This is what separates intelligent, confident people from those who doubt themselves. This is what you must learn too if you are ever to increase your self-confidence in your mental abilities and memory capacity. Shape your brain with positive experiences, put negative experiences into perspective, and make better choices by becoming more self-aware.

A Quick And Easy Daily Routine To Increase Your Brain Power And Your Memory Capacity

Now that you know several techniques with which to increase your brain power and memory capacity, you can put them all together in a simple routine. This chapter will give you a sample routine which you can use as you train your brain for memory improvement.

Start early!

As soon as you wake up in the morning, do some simple stretches. Start with your arms and legs, rotate your shoulders and ankles, and do some hip movement. You can even jog in place for a few seconds, or do a few jumping jacks. Remember that taking care of your body, staying active and fit, is vital if you want to keep your brain sharp.

Breathing exercises help, too.

These breathing exercises should be done regularly throughout the day, especially if you find yourself in rather stressful situations. Simply sit in a comfortable position, and take several deep breaths. With each inhalation, imagine that you are drawing in calm and peace, intelligence and capability. With each exhalation, imagine that you are expelling all doubt, anxiety, and fear from your body.

Keep a journal.

Once you finish exercising, try to remember if you had a dream last night. If you did, write it down in a journal. Try to include as many details as you can remember. It doesn't have to be written in perfect prose, but with practice, you should be able to record your dream in better grammar every day. If you did not have any dreams, you could write down what you were thinking of or doing before you fell asleep.

Eat a healthy breakfast, and a few mental exercises, too.

While you're at it, you can practice recalling the small details by thinking about what you had for breakfast yesterday. If it was a new dish, try to recall the ingredients and the procedure you followed. If you have no idea about the recipe, then try to remember how the meal tasted, and see if your memory can help you detect tell-tale ingredients. Remember that eating good food helps in taking care of your body so that your brain can focus on other things aside from protecting your body from illness.

Afternoons or early evenings are for mental recreation.

Set aside at least twenty minutes every day to do the crossword, play scrabble, complete a jigsaw puzzle, read a book, or play a quick game of chess. Not only does this relieve you from stress, but this also activates other parts of your brain that need to be stimulated.

Record the events of the day in a planner or journal.

This is the simplest way to keep improving your memory. After work, take some time to record everything you can remember about your day. No detail is too small, no event too menial. Did you see interesting people today? Did you notice the stranger sitting next to you on the train? Do you remember what your colleague was wearing?

Writing not only helps you remember and keep track of what happened during the day, but it also aids you in increasing your focus and concentration.

End the day with a few minutes of meditation.

Find a quiet place to meditate just before you go to sleep. Your goal is to remember as much of what happened, to step back and examine your actions, and then to release the stress of the day. At this point, you must remember that you did a good job, and you deserve to rest.

Chapter 10: Brilliant People Work The Work

Consistency and hard work are the two words that define brilliant people. People that work hard learn things faster than the lazy ones.

They are exposed to more experiences, so they learn faster and tend to implement knowledge for the greater good.

They are smart in there, and they mostly end up leaders. They don't give in to what is easy, and they give in to the motivation to achieve something great, regardless of how rough the road may seem to be.

Brilliant people are helpful

Help is the act of adding value to someone else's life. Help might be just spending time with someone that needs a listening ear.

Help can be anything, even the kind of help that comes with a direct profit. The aim is to make people feel encouraged when they spend time with you.

You will begin to understand the social art, and that is when you will be able to leverage the influence you are beginning to create wisely.

Brilliant people solve problems

Your job is to come up with a solution to a problem, and never to get tired of doing the same thing over and over.

Always focus on the problems other people cannot solve, thus everyone will see you as a brilliant one.

You don't need to solve big problems; just focus on the small ones you are good at. The aim is to be solution-oriented and not to be a complainer.

STEPS TO CREATING A BRILLIANT MIND-SET

Fast learning

Effective practice

FAST LEARNING:

There is no going around the fact that you have to learn something before you can apply it in real life. Brilliant people know this, they just get to learn faster than normal people, and they choose the best learning strategies to be ahead of other people.

The regularity

Apart from listening to the news or attending lectures, fast learners study regularly.

Find something interesting and read, even when it means

furthering research about a particular punch word that was used in the new report.

Daily study routine should be implemented as soon as possible to make sure that you use your time wisely.

The more you study, the less time it will take for you to recall things when you need to, and you will be able to apply dynamic knowledge in real life, which means doing things better than normal people.

Find the right context

You can't just study and know everything. Focus on a field, a subject matter of interest.

Research related information about the same subject, the process of what leads to what and so forth.

Allow yourself to get lost in the pool of information searching and you will be surprised how much you learn in a short amount of time.

Experiment with the memorization method

Even if you are not in school memorization is very important for fast recall.

Use the memorization techniques that only uses the acronyms. For example, you can sort out the keyword of every sentence, instead of memorizing the sentence.

Once you remember the keyword, you can construct the sentence in your way. And one way to remember the word is by memorizing the first letter of that word.

You can also classify words according to how they sound or what they define. Let the process be interesting to you.

As you begin this way, in time to come you won't need to arrange words to memorize them, you will just see yourself memorizing things without effort.

Make mind maps

Mindmap is very important in speeding up your learning process especially in the world of technology.

Simply create a visual representation of what you need to recall. Rewrite what you need to remember and look at it for a long time.

You only need to remember how your handwriting looks at that paper to remember what you've written. Grouping and classification of items should also work in this case.

Take a lot of notes

Many people still think taking notes is not important. Nobody is capable of remembering everything without simple revision.

Always take note of things even as you revise them before the occasion you need to remember.

For students, taking notes is very important, even as you find shortcuts to memorizing everything.

Of course, you don't need to write down everything you hear or think, just focus on the keywords and the things you find interesting.

Work on the ambiance

Your environment is very important in implementing any type of learning. Less distraction is always better. It will allow you to concentrate on a single thing until you get hold of the things you need.

Look for a quiet and peaceful place to study, and make sure you switch off your smartphone and computer to get a full concentration.

After doing this once, you will realize that the sacrifice of ignoring friends once in a while and switching off your cell phone for that period does pay off.

Exercise more

Good learners have learned long ago about the power of keeping physically fit.

Studying a lot might bring about fatigue, and laziness might kick-in. Keep your productivity to the rooftop even as you involve in simple exercises such as jogging, yoga, etc.

Accept new information

You have to train your brain to be flexible with new information.

The brain at some point is built to have doubts or simply reject new information. But efficient study comes only when you have a complete focus on the information at hand.

At times you don't need to compare the new information with the old one until you are done digesting the new one.

EFFECTIVE PRACTICE:

Create an atmosphere where the perfect practice will be undertaken. Even though some people prefer silence and total focus to practice what was learned, your stimulation should depend on the motivation achieved over time.

Consistency is very important in this case. You are expected to dwell in an atmosphere that will motivate your morale towards repeating the same thing over and over again until you become perfect in it.

Try as much as possible to get materials that are highly relevant to your work process. You don't need to spend too much time trying to put together things in your work process.

Prepare your body

Do not start a productive practice or study when you are

already stressed. Have a usual ritual that involves doing the things that relax you so that you will be prepared for actual work.

This will also determine the time in which you are going to pursue a particular project.

Your mind also, on the other hand, needs to be prepared for a learning process that involves practicing exactly what you have learned in the first place.

You can start form any technical studies more interesting than your regular practice. Take some coffee if you have to.

Set a goal

Your goal-potential power determines your energy when pursuing something great.

The reputation that is necessary for great practice will only be possible when you have a goal to reach.

You may not be good at what you need to be good at on your first trial.

Your goal should be to be as good as possible. So that you will reach the utmost level of experience needed for a breakthrough.

Split your goals into days. Make sure every day has a singular goal that is required to be achieved.

The speed of your success will depend on the extent to which you can reach that particular goal.

There will be a sudden feeling of accomplishment anytime you reach a particular goal. So you will know that you are making progress while reaching a reasonable goal in life.

Be realistic

You need to recognize the rate at which you learn things. You don't need to do it like the person sitting next to you. Focus on your ability to finish things.

Do you need to start fast?

Can you handle pressure, practicing things at the last minute?

Be realistic with your choices by understanding your true ability actually to finish things on your own.

Smart people become highly brilliant because they make good choices, improving with time even though they are like any other human beings.

Your goals as well need to be realistic as much as possible. You won't need to beat yourself up if you don't achieve your given goal as fast as possible.

Being realistic also means being able to choose goals you can accomplish. Once you can reach smaller goals, reaching bigger goals will be easier.

Identify before you overcome

There is no way you can solve a problem without having a clear identification of what you are dealing with.

Sometimes the problem is never the way you see it. You don't need to power through the process of problem-solving unless you have the assurance that the step you are about to take will yield a definite and beneficial result.

The aim is not to work nonstop but work smart; to benefit by doing the right thing, getting experience and also building your learning capacity.

Even in your studies, you have to focus on what works, get someone to teach you the arithmetic before you spend time on practicing the right thing. Don't spend time on concepts you know you might be wrong about.

Never dwell on the name, dwell on the practice

The fact that you are a pro in something doesn't mean anything in the 21st century.

You need to keep learning regardless of how much you know. You need to put the required work and effort to reach the things that matter.

Also, you need to spend time listening to people that know well.

Apart from the technical application of your study, you need to learn ethics and habits of people greater than you.

Your physical and mental performance will be affected and ultimately the speed at which you gain experience through the required constant practice.

Write on your practice

Keep the work or the practice aside and randomly write down what you have learned so far about a particular subject.

You need to interpret your work process in your language and ignore how it was written by the first instructors.

This is where brilliance and creativity come into play. You will realize that you don't need to learn everything before people will see greatness in you.

Record yourself talking about your experience

This method has been used by artists in practicing what they've learned. The aim is to infuse pride into making sure that you are equipped.

This way you will discover exactly where you are going wrong and improve with time. The tension and confidence should be felt.

It will let you know the level of confidence you have when presenting something you know in public.

Always be in the right state of mind

Your state of mind will define the level of motivation you will achieve even as you recognize the effect from time to time.

Certainty is very important when it comes to showing the ability for creativity. When implementing the things you learned through practice in real work, you should be certain with suggestions before you make changes.

Sometimes you need to switch off completely to allow time for rest. There is no need to keep on moving even when you are weak and tired.

The reward system

Once you put the required work into doing things that matter, you will reap the benefit.

The main thing that matters is how much you reward yourself for doing great.

Consistently remind yourself of how great you are in finishing, memorizing or applying what you have studied.

Even in answering questions, rewarding yourself will give you the real confidence to showcase how great you are.

It makes you feel more appreciated, and you will ultimately experience a confidence boost at a constant ration.

REMEMBER THESE 5 IMPORTANT KEY POINTS

The focus is on everything. Work less, but focus more.

Timing is everything too. Keep track of how much time you spend learning or practicing, and the amount of time you spend doing things that may not contribute to your brilliance.

Don't always trust your memory. Write something down like you won't remember anything. When knowledge and experience begin to accumulate, you will need to write something.

Smarter, not harder. Always look for a smarter way to accomplish your goal, not the harder way. And practicing more will help you achieve a good level of smartness.

Stay on target with a problem-solving model. Never allow yourself to get distracted by other issues in your work process. Focus on the problem at hand and the best ways to reach a definite solution.

Chapter 11: The Fundamental Principles of Speed Reading

Before you begin to learn the methods and strategies that will enable you to become a proficient speed reader, it is important that you first understand what speed reading is all about. Unlike accurate reading or active reading, speed reading is a method of reading that strives to acquire the most important information without getting bogged down in the word by word details of a particular document or piece of written material. Thus, like the skimming reading style, speed reading will enable you to discern important information without having to take the time and effort to read every single word in front of you.

Additionally, you will be able to read the words you need to in a way that is faster and easier than the reading methods you currently use. Therefore, even if you need to do the more in-depth reading, you will be able to do so in as little as one third the time it would take you at your current reading speed.

The first thing to understand about speed reading is that it attempts to restore the ease and speed of reading those pictographic languages afforded its people thousands of years ago. As stated earlier, the advantage of pictographic languages is that they provided whole concepts in single symbols, something that modern languages are largely unable to do.

"Speed reading is the method of reading that helps you to ignore the countless numbers of words that have little to no inherent meaning."

If you stop to consider how many words per sentence you read to contain the important information you will realize that half or more of the words used are largely unnecessary. This means that almost half of the time you spend reading is spent on empty or extraneous words, words that don't deserve the time it takes to read them. While it might take some practice before you get good at being able to pick out the words that matter, the fact is that you will begin to improve your speed immediately once you learn how to read past the unnecessary words and focus on the words that matter.

Another concept of speed reading that is critical to understand is that it removes the editorial element of reading. All too often we can read a written document with a critical eye, one that picks up spelling or grammatical errors. The time and effort it takes to read something with so critical an eye are far more than is necessary. The chances are you aren't grading the piece you are reading. Therefore there is no need to analyze how it is written critically. This is another reason why reading every word with equal attention is counter-intuitive to the whole point of reading, which is to gain a general impression or idea through written words. By reading with the sole purpose of seeing the picture contained in words you will be able to reduce the time it takes you to read any document by a full two-thirds of your current rate.

Finally, it is important to realize the main goal of speed reading. Most people were taught to read by reading out loud. This was a very necessary step as it allowed a teacher to discern if a student was having trouble with any particular aspect of reading. In essence, reading out loud was more for the teacher's benefit than that of the student. Eventually, once the teacher was satisfied that the student could read well, students were told to stop reading out loud. Unfortunately what remained was a voice in the head of the reader pronouncing every word as it was read. Since pronouncing words takes time the overall reading speed of an average person is significantly reduced due to this unnecessary process. Thus, what kills the average person's reading speed is the fact that they make an effort to speak the words in their mind as they read them, a step that is a tragic waste of time and energy.

Speed reading helps a person to remove that element, thus opening their mind to retain more information as well as enabling the person to read any document at least twice as fast by not pronouncing each word in their head.

In the end, speed reading isn't just about helping you to read the same words in less time. Rather, speed reading is about helping you to reinvent the way you read altogether. Instead of seeing the written word as the spoken word spelled out you will begin to see the written word as a source of information that requires only visual recognition. Thus, you will begin to read sentences more like the ancients read pictures, seeing the information rather than the writing process itself. This will prove invaluable for those times when you have large portions of text to read to collect valuable information. Speed reading will help you to reduce the text down to the critical elements alone, while at the same time allowing you to read through the information with speed and purpose, reducing the time and effort it takes to read any item exponentially.

How Speed Reading Can be Beneficial

The very term 'speed reading' suggests the primary function of the methods and strategies presented—to increase the speed with which a person reads. This alone would be valuable for just about anyone. However, the truth of the matter is that proficient speed readers get a lot more than just the ability to read faster.

The mind can act as a sponge of sorts, absorbing everything it sees and hears.

Since the average reader takes the time and effort to read every word written, all the while speaking those words in their mind, this means that the average person's mind tries to soak up every single word that they read. This creates a horrible case of information overload, where the mind is so busy trying to process every word that sometimes the overall meaning of the writing can get lost.

Therefore, when a person applies the methods of speed reading to read past the words and get right to the heart of the information presented, they can retain far more information since their mind isn't bogged down with the task of processing every single word. Thus, not only will speed reading increase a person's reading time, but it will also increase their overall reading comprehension, making them a more effective reader on every level.

While learning to speed read can take as little as 12 hours or less, the more that you continue to practice speed reading, the more it will benefit you. As you develop the techniques for speed reading, you will increase your memory. This is because you will begin to read for the sake of obtaining information rather than simply for the sake of reading. Thus, as you speed read more and more, your mind will develop in a way that will enable you to discern information more quickly and retain it for longer periods. Whether you are reading for work, school or just for pleasure, this is something which will pay rich dividends in the long run. Now, not only will you be able to read faster, you will be able to read smarter as well.

Another way that speed reading can benefit a person is that it can significantly help you to increase your focus. The problem with conventional reading is that the mind can get overwhelmed by the number of words it has to process. This is the problem with reading words rather than information. Once you begin to learn how to read information, your mind will be liberated from the burden of so much useless content contained in any written piece.

By focusing on the important information alone, you will be able to retain an interest in your reading for a longer period. This is because your mind won't become exhausted with the task of processing every word it reads. The longer your mind can stay focused is the more you can read, and the more effective your reading will become. This is particularly beneficial for anyone who is engaged in research projects, where the task of finding relevant information can be taxed under the best of circumstances.

Just as speed reading can increase the speed with which a person reads, as well as their reading comprehension, so too can it increase their ability to think logically.

The mind is like a computer in the sense that it can be programmed to think and act a certain way. Since speed reading can cause the mind to search for valuable information in a more efficient manner while reading it can also help the mind to develop the ability to see things more logically overall. Thus, just as you will be able to discern important information in a written document both quickly and easily, so too will you be able to problem solve in any environment by being able to discern the important information from the mundane and insignificant information surrounding it. This improved logic will increase your intellectual abilities in all areas, making you more valuable in any environment.

Finally, there is the element of confidence and overall peace of mind. As you develop your skills at speed reading, you will discover that you can read and understand more information than ever before in less time than you ever imagined. At first, this may come as a bit of a shock, especially if you were the type who struggled to make passing grades in school. Even so, eventually this increase in academic ability will increase your overall sense of self-confidence and self-worth. This, in turn, will give you greater peace of mind in your current environment, whether at work or school. Additionally, this increase in self-confidence will enable you to take on larger challenges, which can open up all sorts of opportunities that might not have otherwise existed. Thus, not only will you reduce the stress and anxiety of your current condition, but you will improve yourself to the point where you are ready and eager to take on greater things.

How to Prepare for Speed Reading

So far, we have looked at the evolution of writing, different types of reading, and the nature and benefits of speed reading. An understanding of these subjects is essential for anyone who wants to become a proficient speed reader. While anyone can jump into a prescribed set of exercises and improve their reading speed, a person with a deep understanding of the process will experience greater results in less time and with less effort. Now that you have a deeper understanding of the subject, you will be able to achieve your desired results in as little as only 12 hours. The next step of the process, which is equally critical for your success, is the proper preparation for your journey into the world of speed reading.

As with any venture, the better prepared you are, the more likely you will be to succeed. Therefore it is critical to take the time and effort to make sure that you have absolutely everything you need to get the most from the efforts you put into learning how to speed read. The first thing you will need to obtain your desired results in 12 hours or less is the right environment.

Concentration is one of the most critical elements in speed reading.

 Only when you can focus completely on the task at hand will you be able to improve your reading speed along with your reading comprehension.

As you develop your skills, you will doubtlessly be able to speed read effectively even in the most distracting of environments. However, it is essential that you have as little distraction as possible while beginning the learning process. That said, you should find a space where you can practice your speed reading with little to no interruptions. Additionally, there should be a few things within reach that could distract your attention, such as things to fidget with, read or be aware of. Your reading space should be as stark and bare as possible, thus allowing you to focus your complete attention on the material you are reading.

Just as the location where you read is critical to your success, so too, the time of day when you practice speed reading is equally significant. Different people respond to things in different ways. Therefore it is important that you experiment with different times of day to discover which time works best for you. One of the most commonly effective times of day to practice speed reading techniques is first thing in the morning.

For most people the early morning hours are the most peaceful times, allowing for solitude and freedom from interruption. You might want to set your alarm a little earlier to create the necessary time to practice before you have to get ready for your regular day. In the end, even if you have to get up a little earlier, it will be worth it as time you gain will belong completely to you.

Another reason why the early morning is so effective for speed reading exercises is that your mind is fresh, so it is capable of focusing on the task at hand more so than at any other time of day. As the day progresses, you experience more and more things that begin to fill your mind with questions, responses, and even anxieties. Thus, if you wait until the end of the day to practice speed reading, you might find your mind is so full of the day's events that it takes longer to get into the lessons, meaning you get less from your efforts. Again, this is based on common experiences which mean that this may not be as true for you as it is for others. That is why you should take some time to practice regular reading at different times of the day to see which time is the best for you to focus completely on what you are reading.

Finally, there is the matter of mindset. The most common reason why people struggle with learning a new skill or subject is that they lose interest or that their heart isn't really in it, to begin with. Making sure that you stay focused and confident on your goal of increasing your reading speed and comprehension is essential if you are to succeed in this program.

Take the time to remind yourself during every day of the hopes and ambitions you have with regards to speed reading. Constantly encourage yourself to succeed at your next speed-reading exercise.

By just taking the odd moment here and there during the day to give yourself such encouragement you will prepare yourself mentally and psychologically for your next lesson. When you create the right mindset, you set yourself up for a level of success that cannot be achieved any other way.

Essential Tools Needed for Speed Reading

Once you have established the right environment, the right time and the right mindset for your journey into the world of speed reading, you need to make sure that you have all the essential tools that the journey requires. These tools are mostly basic items, many of which you will already have. Even if you don't have an exact tool that is recommended it is likely that you will be able to substitute it with something that you already possess. This means that you should be able to achieve your goal of increasing your reading speed and reading comprehension in 12 hours or less without any additional expense or hassle.

The first thing you will need is a reliable timepiece. Many speed reading programs will recommend that you use a stopwatch, as this is the ideal way in which you can keep track of how long it takes you to read a particular passage. Having a stopwatch or a timer with an alarm is very beneficial for most exercises, as this allows you to focus solely on the reading without having to keep an eye on the time. Again, if you don't have a stopwatch or a timer with an alarm, don't panic.

There is every chance that you do and don't realize it! Take a look in your kitchen to see if you have an egg timer or something similar.

Many kitchens have small timer gadgets floating around in the junk drawer, and this is all that you need to keep track of your reading time. If you don't have a timer of any kind, you can always use your microwave or oven timer. Simply set the timer for the duration you need and make sure that you are in a place where you can hear the alarm when it goes off. If you want an actual timer, and you have the cash for one, then you can find a reliable timer at just about any store including grocery stores, office supply stores or general retail stores.

Another tool you will need is a pointer. Fortunately, this can come in any form shape or size. Using a pen, a pencil or even your finger will suffice for exercises requiring a pointer. The important thing is that you find an item that is comfortable to hold and that doesn't attract your attention visually.

As you develop your skills at speed reading, you will want to keep track of your progress. Having a small notebook designated for your speed reading exercises is highly recommended. This will give you a place to record your reading times, as well as a place to write down the answers to any questions your exercises ask.

There will be times when you need to test your reading comprehension, so you will want to write your answers down in those instances. Additionally, having a notebook will give you a place to write down any specific questions, goals or ideas that you have along the way. Again, this is a journey of sorts, and each person takes this journey in their unique way.

Therefore it is very important to personalize this journey in every way possible.

List your ambitions, your obstacles and any other information that will help you to achieve your overall goal.

Finally, there is the matter of reading material. While this book contains some practice passages to use at first, these will only be effective for so long. After a few uses, the information in the passages will begin to sink in, creating a familiarity with the information that is counter-intuitive to the exercises. Thus, you will need to make sure that you have multiple sources of reading material that can keep you stocked with fresh passages for your speed reading practice.

The materials you use can come in any form. However, it is recommended that you have some materials in physical form, as these will be easier to use for certain exercises. Eventually, you will be able to integrate digital materials, using your laptop or desktop or even your smartphone for your daily speed reading exercises, but newspapers, magazines or print books will be required at the beginning.

Conclusion

The more we learn about the intricacies of the brain and its vital role in our daily existence, the more fascinated we are about how such a small organ could represent everything about the person that we are.

We've realized that, like the heart, which never tires of pumping lifeblood since the day we were born, the brain is as tireless, continually keeping us aware of our environment, enabling us to make intelligent decisions, and helping us learn from experiences so that we can come out of situations always a better human being.

Being able to make memories is undeniably one of the essential functions of the brain. It is in being ready to commit to memory and being able to remember and recall that we can make meaningful relationships with other people. It is in recognizing that we can appreciate ourselves and understand our place in the grand scheme of things.

Lastly, if you enjoyed this book I ask that you please take the time to review it on Audible.com. Your honest feedback would be greatly appreciated.

Thank you.

Now, I would like to share with you a free sneak peek to

another one of my books that I think you will really enjoy. The book is called "NLP: The Ultimate Guide to Manipulation" Published by Joe Karlins and Marvin Navarro.

It's A Practical Guide to Master Body Language Techniques and learn how to Influence People with Persuasion. You will also Learn How to Analyze People's Emotions and Master Neurolinguistic at Work and for Seduction.

Enjoy!

Introduction

You will find many NLP models that will help you in every aspect of your life and career. The approach you will find is practical, you will see results and it is growing in influence in many different disciplines.

Since NLP is constantly growing and evolving and this book is static, it will work as a snapshot of NLP. Even though things may be different tomorrow, it doesn't mean that the practice in this book won't be helpful.

You should view this information as a stepping stone. It is giving you a chance to explore a new area and to keep your life exciting. This book is meant for the beginner to easily understand what to do without confusion.

NLP is a state of mind and a way of being. NLP is something practical that has to be done. While reading about it will teach you a lot, you have to actively practice it to reap any benefits. You will find sets of models, techniques, and skills that will change the way you act and think. This is meant to be useful and to improve your life.

You have to find out what works by doing it. Then you can figure out what didn't work and then work with that until you are able to make it work. This is the great thing about NLP. Let's get started.

Introduction to NLP

A person's behavior is based on specific structures. With NLP or Neuro-Linguistic Programming, the way that people act, speak, and think is examine with models. Richard Bandler has patterned these models. In the beginning, he patterned his work after characters like Virginia Stair, Fritz Perls, and Milton Erickson, who were seen to have amazing behavioral and linguistic abilities.

Your own experiences are the main uses of the NLP system. There is no way to learn NLP through sequential steps and techniques. However, programmers become skilled at using methods to change how the brain functions and perceives. Its goal is to create a good foundation of attitude and skill so that they can produce new techniques and approaches to self-preserve.

You aren't going to only depend on steps and techniques that are taught to you. You are going to learn how to create new steps so that you can continually achieve success. It works as an investigation of knowledge that will use different stage of human attitude and development, as well as thought formation.

It is going to give you effective tools and strategies that will define who you are, the role you play, and your ideal state of success. While the initial state begins with you, the process will involve all of those around you and the environment to create the best mindset.

The purpose behind NLP is to work as a toolbox of thoughts, skills, and attitudes. The models will become patterns through which your habits will change and be redefined. When you plan on using NLP, you are aiming for personal development and success.

NLP can also make you successful. Whether you are faced with problems in your family, work, or leisure, NLP will give you the ability to alter your outlook and view towards the world. You will start to notice the important meaning of life and what priorities are important in your life. Once you are able to find your strong and weak areas, you will be able to focus on what will make you successful and efficient.

NLP will also improve communication. Positive thinking is able to be changed into words. You will end up becoming more verbally competent when you learn how to change your thoughts and emotions and the way you share perspectives and how you communicate with others. Communication is an amazing method that will give you a better influence, a larger network of friends, and a better way to express yourself.

NLP will also bring together the mind, body, and emotions. There are a lot of people who experience difficulty putting all of the plans into actionable steps. Other people aren't able to learn from their experiences. When these things happen, it means that your mind, body, and emotions aren't working together. Through the use of NLP, you will be able to make connections with each aspect of your existence. NLP will allow all of these aspects to work together so that you can reach success.

To help explain NLP, let's take a look at the history. NLP was first created in the '70s by Richard Bandler and John Grinder. This development was created at the University of California and supervised by Gregory Bateson. Bandler, Bateson, and Grinder were influenced by Alfred Korzybski because of his theories surrounding human presuppositions and modeling. Other contributors to the theory were Leslie Cameron-Bandler, David Gordon, Judith DeLozier, and Robert Dilts.

Grinder and Bandler worked on the NLP theory until they had a falling out in the '80s. Ginder and DeLozier later created the New Code which took a mind and body approach. Bandler's approach looked at Ericksonian submodalities and hypnosis. Michael Hall mainly looked at mental states and neuro-semantics.

Ted James looked at the best periods of life for therapy and Anthony Robbins made use of products that use NLP. At this point, NLP had been managed and created in different independent sectors. It had also grown and been renamed several times over. Then again, it has also suffered from a lack of definition and regulation.

After many different legal battles, legally, NLP has now become a generic term. Even after all of these years, NLP practitioners still don't have an agreement in regard to the theory. That's why a lot of people have abused it. Still, a lot of the work is dependent on the ideas of the co-developers and other such individuals. For a person to formally practice NLP for human development and condition, they will need to become certified.

Why is it called Neuro-Linguistic Programming? "Neuro" refers to the brain, which what controls your behavior and actions and it stores your memories and experiences. "Linguistic" comes from the word language. This means the "neuro-linguistic" refers to how language affects the brain. Non-verbal cues, words, and symbols are able to cause a response. "Programming" is used to describe the mechanism that is analogous to a computer program.

There are presuppositions of Neuro-Linguistic Programming. The NLP foundation comes with a few basic presuppositions. Every technique, model, and strategy that is connected to NLP is used along with these assumptions. Since NLP studies the subjective experience, an assumption would be that people can determine objective reality.

The perfect or best direction for life is non-existent. This is the reason why a person can only reach the best possible moment and hope that they have the correct attitude to make the best choices. A person's objective in using NLP is to find excellence and wisdom. Once you widen your choices, you will also be improving your odds of finding excellence. When you are able to acquire different views of the environment, you will gain wisdom.

A territory and a map are not the same things. You can't live your life with only one direct route. Humans are given several different options on the ways that they can live their lives. Depending on what your experiences and perceptions are, you will make decisions that you take you on different paths.

You are in possession of a map to your reality, which will involve a representation of you and those around you. With this map, you will be able to react to the world and be able to better understand yourself. However, if you end up having too much discrepancy between your personal map and territory, you could end up getting lost.

Your life and mind work in systematic processes. There is always going to be an interaction between two people or between a person and the environment. Everything within the universe is connected to each other. When something in your mind or life is affected, your whole experience will absorb what happens. This connection is needed to keep a constant balance.

Communication elicits a response and it comes with a meaning. The manner and content of the reply you receive from the person you are communicating with is the point of your communication. Even if you are aiming to deliver a certain message, validation of understanding can only happen when one person has responded properly.

For example, if you are telling a joke and the person you were telling it to didn't laugh or understand it, then the manner of your telling of the joke didn't help your expected response.

There are two levels of communication — conscious and unconscious. Verbal communication is only one form of communication. A lot of people aren't aware of the fact that they use a lot of body language, facial expressions, posturing, hand and eye movements, and non-verbal cues while they are talking. People are even able to add to the tone and mood of the conversation to relay the message more effectively. Take the statement, "Get out of here." This statement can be communicated in several different ways that could relay a positive or negative message.

Communication can't fail, it only gets an outcome. A person can't say that their communication was useless or was a failure if they didn't get the response they wanted. All it means is that the result ended up being different than what they had expected. This should influence the person to enhance their skills and attitude in regards to communication. You must learn from unpleasant outcomes so that you can identify and gauge the things that kept you from sending out the correct message.

Rapport, which we talk in depth about later on, relates to people according to their world. Each person is able to make their own model or representation of the world that are based on their understanding of environmental influences and previous experiences. This is the reason why you will need to exert some effort if you want to create a new model.

It's important that you are able to see the world as others do so that you can build rapport and communicate effectively. If you keep your mind close in regards to their representation, you will likely have a very hard time getting the response you are looking for. Other people could have a hard time understanding your model.

If a communicator is inflexible, it will be seen through their resistance. When you find that the person you are talking with is resistant, this doesn't mean that they are closed off to the communication. It could mean that you have established rapport. Thus, you will need to enter into their world model. Otherwise, they won't be able to unconsciously receive your message. You also need to learn how you can become flexible so that you are able to understand and speak their language. This is especially true because they can't understand yours. You could end up insulting them without knowing it if you aren't flexible.

You don't have to obtain new things just so that you can be a good leader or communicator. You don't have to obtain new things to create positive changes. You have everything that you already need. All of the mental, emotional, and behavioral resources are within you.

If you aren't able to see them, then you haven't created an access to them. You are not aware of your strengths. You could have a lot of chronic stressors that will keep you from using them. Through NLP, you will be able to be more aware of the resources you have and learn how to correctly use them.

Your positive worth will stay the same even if your internal and external behavior is in question. All humans have worth and dignity no matter what their thoughts and actions are. Then there are good and bad behaviors that will determine their judgment of worth to themselves and the environment.

Your value won't change no matter how bad you act. The value of your actions and behavior are measured based on the expectations of those around you. You are able to change your bad actions and manners so that you can come into alignment with your values.

Every behavior is meant to have a good outcome. However, not every behavior is supposed to be done with positive manners. There are self-preserving mechanisms that are meant for personal benefits. The process of this goal can be dangerous for you and others. These types of behaviors could be unconscious. Your mind and body have a tendency to think about a positive outcome and end up neglecting negative manners.

You have to make sure that you don't rush into decisions or actions without getting the information that you need. You also need to make sure that you take the time to calm down. Disrupted emotions and haste will often cause inadequacy in your actions and bad judgment. You have to be able to differentiate automated and conscious responses. You also need to be able to see the difference between ideals and realities. You should give yourself a reality check every now and again so that you can up your odds of making the best decision.

The process of NLP assimilates subjective experiences. Ever since the moment you started to remember your life events, your brain has worked tirelessly to store information. This information is then recalled through memories and experiences that are changed into personal beliefs and perceptions. These beliefs could be negative or positive depending on how you react to your previous experiences. Positive beliefs can be kept and negative ones can be replaced by positive ones.

NLP works by changing your false or negative understandings. When you are able to connect your brain to your senses, you will find that you can let go of negative feelings, vague thoughts, and traumatic experiences. You have the power to get rid of whatever is hindering you from living a successful and happy life.

For NLP to be effective, every part needs to work together. The first part is the neurological aspect. Your nervous system will take in your experiences using the five senses — smell, taste, touch, hearing, and sight. Your nervous system will then send out signals to the brain so that you can make sense of them.

Then you have the language aspect. This includes verbal and non-verbal communication. These systems of communication order and code your neural representations to provide them meaning. The last part is programming. This is your brain's ability to organize the information from each system. The organization is the way that you achieve specific results and goals. When all three systems are used in unison, you will get a synergistic effect. This allows you to get your desired results.

NLP will help you to perform several different functions. As I have said, it will help your communication skills. NLP can be used to create behavioral changes in others and ourselves. It will provide you with different perspectives of the outside world. These new perspectives will help you to adjust your behaviors and attitudes.

Through NLP, you will become more aware of the things you

do. Most people don't pay attention to their actions and thoughts. NLP provides you with a process that will keep you grounded and in control.

Everybody sees the world through different filters. These filters will use different beliefs and values. NLP can help you get rid of these filters. This will give you a better view of the other person's point of view. It will also give you the ability to understand how your actions will affect the lives of others.

NLP is able to create a real difference. You will find improved information. You are able to use this improved information to make the best decisions. The better decisions will bring you better actions. Better actions will give you better results.

Thank you for reading, this preview is now over.

I hope you enjoyed this preview of my book "NLP 2.0 Mastery - How to Analyze People" Published by John Clark.

Please make sure to check out the full book on Amazon.com

Thank you for reading.